Family
OE

Family OE

Luke & Karen
Williamson

*A really useful Kiwi guide to
travelling overseas with your children*

NEW
HOLLAND

First published in 2008 by New Holland Publishers (NZ) Ltd
Auckland • Sydney • London • Cape Town

www.newhollandpublishers.co.nz

218 Lake Road, Northcote, Auckland 0627, New Zealand
Unit 1, 66 Gibbes Street, Chatswood, NSW 2067, Australia
86–88 Edgware Road, London W2 2EA, United Kingdom
80 McKenzie Street, Cape Town 8001, South Africa

Publishing manager: Matt Turner
Editor: Renée Lang
Cover and internal design: Halcyon Design
Front and back cover photographs: Karen Williamson

National Library of New Zealand Cataloguing-in-Publication Data

Williamson Luke.
Family OE : a really useful Kiwi guide to travelling overseas with
your children / Luke & Karen Williamson.
Includes bibliographical references and index.
ISBN 978-1-86966-185-4
1. Children—Travel—Guidebooks. 2. Vacations—Guidebooks.
I. Williamson, Karen. II. Title.
910.41—dc 22

10 9 8 7 6 5 4 3 2 1

Colour reproduction by Pica Digital Pte Ltd, Singapore
Printed in China at Everbest Printing Co, on paper sourced from sustainable forests.

This book is dedicated to Isaac
and Pearl, two fantastic and brave
travelling companions.

The Master in the art of living makes little distinction between his work and his play, his labour and his leisure, his mind and his body, his education and his recreation, his love and his religion. He hardly knows which is which. He simply pursues his vision of excellence in whatever he does, leaving others to decide whether he is working or playing. To him he is always doing both.

Zen Buddhist text

Contents

Greece. This is the sort of astounding sight you can look forward to on your trip – Meteora with its monasteries perched on seemingly impossible peaks. Even the children could appreciate these church visits, although it was the three-legged kitten that most captured their attention.

(Right) Loaded up and ready to leave Athens, on our way to Delphi, Greece. The photo was taken by Lesley Immink, the Imminks being the only other family we came across who were doing a trip similar to ours – and of course they were Kiwis.

Introduction

This book has come about because not only did we want to do the big overseas experience (OE) with our kids, but we got past talking about it and actually did it. And now that we have safely returned, we'd like to share our experience with anyone who's considering taking their children travelling and who might benefit from what we learned along the way. We're not talking about a couple of weeks package holiday on an island somewhere or a shopping excursion to Australia. Oh, no. We're talking the full monty – the big OE!

In our case there were four of us: Luke, Karen and our children Isaac and Pearl, 11 and eight years old respectively. Travelling via private car and various forms of public transport, we visited 10 countries including the UK, several countries in Mediterranean Europe, plus Turkey and Canada. All up, we slept in 96 different beds. While this book relates to our travels in the above countries, the principles and advice that follow are designed for application to family travel in general.

Karen's dissatisfaction with her job and my need for a break in routine were the factors that kick-started our travel adventure. We were ready to go overseas again, but this time we wanted to take the children with us. The timing of the trip was critically balanced: the children would be old enough to enjoy the trip and be as self-reliant as possible, but with Isaac still 11 years old we could enjoy a year of travel before he hit adult fares. We wanted to spend quality time together as a family while the children were still children. We had learnt through friends that the family dynamics would change when the kids hit their teens, and we hoped that the bonding experience of the big trip would help us get through the potential difficulties ahead in young adulthood.

Karen and I were eager to get back to Europe after a break of 20-odd years, and were excited about showing the children some of the 'big stuff' out in the world: the Colosseum, the Eiffel Tower, and so on. We also believed that a year of travelling would improve the children's educational opportunities rather than hinder them. We wanted them to feel a sense of history, to gain perspective on how they fit into the world, to develop their abilities to think for themselves, and to gain confidence. And on a purely personal level, after 15 years of running my own business I was looking forward to having a decent break from work (and the rat race in general) and to soaking up some alternative culture.

Although our original plan was to be away from home for up to 12 months this was cut, for various reasons, to eight months. During this time there were, we're glad to say, no tragedies: just one inconvenient incident, a few minor traumas and very little illness. All in all, the trip was a resounding success, but we certainly could have done with some practical guidance along the lines of what's on offer within these pages.

The first thing to understand is that there is not necessarily a right or wrong way of planning a major trip that involves children. Families come in all shapes and sizes but the advice given here is based on our personal experience, gained mostly through the school of trial and error, so feel free to accept what sounds as if it will work for you and discard what won't, i.e. be flexible. So much will depend on the age of your children – you know what they are capable of doing and enjoying, so adapt our suggestions accordingly. As Captain Barbossa says in *Pirates of the Caribbean*, 'they're more what you'd call "guidelines" than actual rules'. Our real aim is to motivate you to go on your own family OE.

Money is obviously an important issue. People thought that we must be really wealthy, or that one of us at least had to be a neurosurgeon or the head of a giant corporation, to be able to travel so far and for so long. This is *so* not true. However, we did have a fairly manageable mortgage so we simply extended it to cover the cost of the trip. This might not appeal or even be practicable for most other people, but it's not the purpose of this book to tell you how to raise the money; rather it's how to make the most of the trip, whichever way you may choose to finance it.

Regarding our children's education, Karen and I have a philosophy that has been heavily influenced by our time at Playcentre, which focuses on 'parents as first teachers'. We have carried this approach right through and while this reference is not intended as a plug for Playcentre, it may help readers to understand the relationship we have with our children.

When someone says to us, 'You're so lucky to have done a trip like that', I can tell you that luck had nothing to do with it! It was all about planning, dedication to the cause, and a great deal of hard work. We never thought of this trip as a 'holiday'.

A word now on remaining positive. Much of this book's content deals with some of the difficulties that might be encountered on a family OE and, of course, tips on how to overcome them, because this is what we figure will be most helpful. That doesn't mean you should anticipate a series of negative experiences. Far from it! The huge benefits from a trip such as the one we took made us incredibly happy and grateful that we did it, but these benefits can also be intangible, and therefore harder to express in written form. So if you're serious about doing it, then take it from us that it'll be worth every cent and sacrifice.

Although we've written this book from the point of view of parents, we appreciate that other adults may well be involved, e.g. grandparents, a member of the extended family, a caregiver, a guardian or perhaps a trusted friend. Whatever the case, when we refer to 'parents' please take that to mean accompanying adult/s.

And finally we'd like it to go on record that this book is very much a collaboration of ideas and effort from Karen and me. Occasionally, too, we have solicited contributions from our friend and fellow New Zealander Lesley Immink, whom we met along with her husband and children while they were in Greece, also part-way through a grand family OE. It was a meeting that resulted in our two families becoming very good friends, and their comments and suggestions regarding the contents of this book have been much appreciated.

It's our fervent hope that after reading this book you'll be inspired to take your family overseas. And if you have any queries that haven't been specifically addressed within these pages, feel free to drop us an e-mail (klip@halcyondesign.co.nz).

If you plan for some travel perfection, there's a good chance you'll find some of it somewhere along the way.

(Right) You need to find that balance between a well-planned trip and being spontaneous.

Chapter 1:
Planning the trip

There are definite pros and cons to planning well in advance. One advantage is that you can give plenty of notice of your intention to interested parties, e.g. your boss, extended family and friends. Another is the opportunity it presents to start saving as well as researching the trip at your leisure. Disadvantages include the risk of any or all of you getting impatient as the months – and possibly years – tick by. There is also the possibility that some other factor – such as career or health – could change your lives to a point where you might have to give up or put on hold your planned expedition.

When my father was diagnosed with terminal cancer, he said to Karen: 'Don't waste your life on shit . . . don't spend time with people you don't like just because you think you should, and don't do things that you hate.' Inspirational words, and just the fuel she needed to get that travel momentum going again.

Finding airfares to suit your budget and schedule is one of many challenges you will face. Consider also the time of year you'll be away – you really need to book ahead for busy seasons in popular locations, e.g. summertime in any of the main European cities. It's not that you'll necessarily miss out on accommodation, it's just that you'll have to pay a premium for it, even more than the usual frightening prices. Now that you can book most, if not all, aspects of travel on the Internet, take advantage of this whenever possible.

We booked our visits to several key tourist destinations such as the London Eye before we left home. It's even possible to book a time to visit the Uffizi Art Museum in Florence, Italy, and beat the queues!

Although paying via the Internet for accommodation many months and many miles away can take some getting used to, there are secure ways of going about it as long as you practise safe banking. We suggest that you assess each situation as it arises (consult with your bank if you need advice on payment methods). Another useful tip is to print out a record of your booking, e.g. a return e-mail confirming you've booked and paid for a stay in a particular place, and take them with you as proof.

Booking in advance may help you beat the queues at tourism icons, such as the Louvre in Paris.

If you plan to book through an agent, choose carefully and get to know him/her well. Agents often know of tricks and savings that you wouldn't find in books or on the Internet.

All of our on-line accommodation bookings were made by direct credit, PayPal or international money order. Every one was secure and honoured by the host.

Use the months prior to leaving as valuable learning time. Stock up on travel guides and documentary DVDs/videos from your local library and plan for the whole family to watch any travel-related programmes on TV that might be suitable. You'll find you can spend many enjoyable evenings poring over guide books, maps and Internet sites.

Our kids particularly enjoyed learning about different countries through videos, DVDs and TV programmes as it involved screen time, normally strictly rationed in our household.

Goals

We thoroughly recommend setting up some family objectives, e.g. the main one is likely to be along the lines of 'to have a wonderful adventure that includes lots of quality family time'. Not everyone's cup of tea, but it is valuable in terms of clarifying what you hope to achieve on the trip. It is also important if you feel that this might be a one-off, never-to-be-repeated-in-the-near-future trip and you want to maximise the benefits. It doesn't have to be written or formal; it may be just a discussion together over dinner. Getting something verbal from your children is likely to be easier than obtaining written goals.

Itinerary

This is the time to make your dreams come true. And while you'll probably have to allow for budget and time constraints, and the occasional geographical/political barrier, now is the time to do it rather than talk about it.

Deciding on where your family is going to travel can also be very exciting for children because in this part of the planning they can have great fun coming up with dream locations – and have a real chance of one or more of their choices coming to fruition!

We chose to travel within the UK and Mediterranean Europe for several reasons: the close proximity of countries, the relative ease and low cost of getting from one to another, the high density of sightseeing highlights in this region, and the low risk of language difficulties.

Take advantage of friends and family

Make a list of extended family or friends with whom you might be able to stay while you are away. E-mail them to introduce – or reintroduce – yourself and let them know when you will be in their part of the world. In many cases you'll already know when it's OK to ask outright for a room for the night while at other times you may need to fish for an offer. It's always a good idea to be very clear about how many of you will be staying and how long you'd like to stay. Meeting overseas relatives can give children a real sense of where a family comes from and give them a sense of belonging in the world, rather than just the country they live in. They can learn a lot, too, about how others live from being immersed in their lifestyle, if only for a short time.

On our arrival at Karen's cousin's place in England, Karen drew a family tree in her journal so both children could make sense of how all these people they had just met were related to them and to each other. After the warm welcome they received, both children now feel like they hold a place in the extended family.

Obviously, staying with family (or friends for that matter) from time to time will be advantageous in terms of saving on accommodation costs.

But there are also benefits such as being welcome in someone's home plus the chance of meeting and talking to locals that could well lead to discovering places that may not feature in guide books or websites. These opportunities can be among the defining and most fondly remembered moments of your trip. Chances are your hosts will end up visiting you one day, at which time you can reciprocate their kindness.

We had many wonderful experiences meeting people whom we already knew from a previous visit as well as those we met for the first time. We have a family joke, to the effect that you don't invite the Williamsons to stay unless you mean it. And thanks to our forwardness in inviting ourselves to stay, we also forged some long-lasting friendships including a family in Liverpool, the father of which Karen got to know through her involvement in an online photographic community. When she told him we would be visiting the UK he joked that he would buy her a Guinness, but we ended up meeting him and his wife in Snowdonia National Park, Wales, and then again in Liverpool where we had the best night out at the Cavern Club while their teenage daughter babysat our kids! We are now good friends, but the point is that we would never have met them had we not had the gall to invite ourselves into their lives.

The four seasons

Choosing the best time of year during which to travel can depend on many things, including how long you intend to be away. If you're going to Europe, then spring is always a good time of year to visit, not least because accommodation costs are lower than in summer, sometimes just half the summer holiday price.

We left New Zealand at the end of our summer (April) in order to arrive in Europe for the northern spring and summer. We also wanted to see some of the bigger cities, such as Paris, Barcelona, Lisbon and London, before they were overrun with tourists in summer.

Summer, however, has the benefits of hot (most of the time, you hope!) weather and plenty of action. Visitor sites in the UK and Europe are usually open longer, there are lots of shows, concerts, festivals and exhibitions, and everyone – visitors and locals alike – tends to be in that joyous mood that summer usually brings. It's also a great time to travel further north and do some sightseeing during more user-friendly temperatures. Even up north, though, you won't escape the crowds and rising costs. Everything – especially accommodation – gets busy and expensive and you will have to plan your way through it as best you can. Our advice is to get up early, find the bargains, book in advance – in other words, do whatever it takes.

In some countries good accommodation rates can be available during autumn (although not as low as spring rates) and more often than not there's plenty of lovely, lingering late-summer weather at that time of year. Occasionally, though, it can be bloody cold and miserable, but as you can't control the weather, you just have to make the most of it – or move country. (Italy seems to defy the trends a bit and be expensive year-round, excluding, curiously, August when the whole country goes on holiday in order to escape the heat in the cities so prices for accommodation decrease.)

Travelling during a European winter can be tricky because although prices are a lot lower at that time of year, many places are closed for the duration. Don't avoid winter just for the sake of it though, as there are lots of good cold-weather experiences to be had, e.g. superb skiing and Sweden's Ice Hotel.

For an indication of what the weather is typically like at a particular time of year in those countries you intend to visit, have a look at www.bbc.co.uk/weather/world/city_guides/

Given a 'three months in Europe' time frame, we would recommend a spring/summer combo. For a longer trip, say six months, we suggest going in spring/summer/autumn and then you'll get a bit of everything – from Mediterranean summer nights to cosy English pubs in cold weather. Lovely!

How long?

We would recommend six months as being the optimum length of time to be away with your family (based on the assumption that you'll be tourists for the duration with no plans to work). Three months is also good, but you will probably return wishing that you had stayed away longer – not necessarily a bad thing if you can afford to go back again in the not-too-distant future.

After eight months on the road, our family was physically and financially exhausted. The kids were keen to be home for Christmas so we booked our flights and headed home a bit earlier than we had originally intended when we planned the trip.

When you're constantly on the move, especially with young children, it can be very tiring. One way to overcome this problem is to allow for rest stops of a week or more (we called them 'anchor points') during which you make a point of staying in one place for that period. You'll find being able to unpack and relax for a few days without the constant worry of having to find suitable restaurants or accommodation in yet another strange place hugely beneficial. In hindsight we wish we'd had more of these, but it can be a difficult balance to strike given that there are so many interesting places to see and people to meet. It's probably better to do less and do it better.

Consider pre-booking apartment accommodation for rest stops. You'll really enjoy having a bit more space – especially after the shoebox-sized accommodation you're likely to have experienced up to this stage. We found www.holiday-rentals.co.uk to have an excellent selection of apartments and houses to rent, as did www.ownersdirect.co.uk

Another way of doing this trip would be to get four or five longer-term apartment rentals in your chosen, favourite destinations, and do short adventures out from these 'bases'. This would give you the opportunity to get to know the area around your base well, and not get quite so worn out from constant travelling. You would just need to balance these positives against whether you got to see all the things you wanted to and making

sure the children didn't get bored with being in one place too long.

If you are considering working during your trip, be aware of difficulties that include administrative delays; choosing a location; finding short-term, fully-furnished accommodation; and what to do with the children all day – it's not easy to just drop them into school.

The village of Loutro on the Greek island of Crete was one of our 'anchor points'. Loutro can only be accessed by boat or on foot, and made for an idyllic and peaceful one-week rest stop.

Time off work

Not everyone can take extended leave from work. You have to decide how important the trip is to you and your family, and then be prepared to fight for the leave required. It may happen that you're pleasantly surprised – an enlightened employer will be aware that they will regain an employee full of enthusiasm and new ideas. You'll never know until you ask.

Some people might decide to just quit their job, go on their adventure and then come back to a fresh start. This will be an attractive option for those who've been craving a major change. But if you are worried about losing your place on the corporate ladder, this could be your opportunity to assess how committed you are to fighting your way to the top. Let's face it, no one has ever been heard to say on their deathbed, 'Gee, I wish I'd spent more time at the office.' You can keep putting off doing the things you would love to do because of the pressures of work and mortgage, but you might just find that the chance has passed you by and, particularly, the chance to experience it with your children. Hopefully, this book will convince you that travelling with your family is an opportunity too good to miss.

Booking in advance

How much you want to plan and book in advance will vary depending on your personal preferences; however, if you're planning to be away at peak holiday time, i.e. summer, it would pay to have some bookings in place rather than leave too much to chance.

We pre-arranged about 30% of the trip and organised the remaining 70% as we went along. As we were going to be in Europe over spring and summer we chose to book ahead for our time in London (and the London Eye), Paris and Barcelona, and for a two-week holiday cottage in France's Dordogne region.

Don't assume that accommodation will be freely available at quieter times of the year because hotels and other kinds of accommodation can be known to close down altogether from late autumn through to early spring. If you're planning on staying at hostel-style accommodation and you are happy to book as you go, then we recommend using websites such as www.hostels.net and www.hostelbookers.com to book. Another advantage is that many hostels offer budget options for sightseeing.

Leaving where you are going to stay up to a whim of the moment can raise stress levels in some instances, but it can also be a pleasant relief from constantly organising accommodation in advance. It also allows you the luxury of choosing between various options once you get to a destination, rather than booking sight unseen. Then, if you wish, you will also be at liberty to stay for a few extra days. Some of your best adventures could well come from these kinds of impromptu arrangements if you're the kind of family that is comfortable about leaving things loose. We all know of people who love to make things up as they go along while others need the reassurance of a schedule set in concrete. You'll know which is right for you, but do bear in mind that children may need more security than you in order to enjoy themselves. They will not always take kindly to waiting around for hours in a strange city while their parents try to find a room for the night.

Booking ahead is advisable if your plan is to visit a town or region during a particular event such as a festival, religious holiday or similar. This will put accommodation in very short supply, so it pays to find out what events are scheduled for the period you will be there. That way, you'll be sure of a bed as well as the opportunity for you and your family to enjoy taking part in a valuable cultural experience.

We arrived via train in the historic Italian town of Martina Franca one autumn afternoon after spending the day and previous night travelling. It was our first night in Italy and, as we didn't have any accommodation booked, we headed to the tourism office – a 15-minute walk uphill from the train station. We were all pretty tired – and soon pretty upset – to discover it was closed until 6 pm. On top of that, it was getting cold and dark, the kids were hungry and Isaac really wanted that first Italian pizza experience he had been promised 12 months ago – a big drawcard to lure him into travelling in the first place. I waited in the square with the kids while Karen wandered Martina Franca's old town, a maze of cobbled alleyways with no sign of a hostel, pension or B&B of any kind. All the shops were closed and there was no one on the street to ask for help. Eventually we found a hotel; it was more expensive than we'd budgeted for, but the staff were friendly and let us have a dinner of chicken and beer on their deck. We had no time or energy left for enjoying Martina Franca and remember this experience with less than fond memories, simply because we didn't book ahead. Isaac did eventually get his pizza.

On the flipside, we arrived in Dieppe, France, late one afternoon and found that we had missed the ferry to England. Caught out, we had to try to find some affordable accommodation on this, the first weekend of the school holidays. Oops! The information office on the waterfront told us that just about everything within our budget was booked out. However, as we had a car, they were able to recommend a delightful B&B up the coast a short way and which, because it was out of town, was very reasonable pricewise. We made the 20-minute trip through stunning countryside and found ourselves at a gorgeous big homestead in a tiny village, being welcomed by Sylvie, the bonny, smiling, apron-wearing French hostess. We got a beautiful room with a double bed and bunks for the children, drinks and conversation after we had settled in (more good practice for my French) and, next day, one of our best breakfasts of the entire trip – coffee, juice, cereal, fresh bread, home-made chocolate gateau, fresh fruit, home-made jams, yoghurt, ham and cheese! So, sometimes it pays to just go with the flow.

Housekeeping issues

How you choose to finance your trip is up to you, but should you decide to rent out your house to help with ongoing income, here are some of the practical elements involved in this option, e.g. furniture storage, choosing the right tenants, length of rental period and the appointment of either a professional property manager or a trusted person to look after house-related matters while you are away.

We chose to finance our big adventure by increasing the mortgage on our home and then renting it out in our absence – not everyone is able to do this, let alone be comfortable with the prospect, but it worked for us. If you choose to save up all the funds for your trip, you will need to allow for that in your planning time. For those who have the funds available without having to resort to borrowing, good for you!

Storage is an issue. If you're not fortunate enough to have relatives with spare space, there are many commercial storage units available and the Internet or *Yellow Pages* will help you find a suitable place. Storage costs vary according to the amount of space and the time period required. Be aware that your insurance company must be informed of the circumstances as your possessions will be covered only if the place of storage is 'approved'.

If you decide to rent out your house, and you want to know more about what's involved, visit www.dbh.govt.nz/tenancy-index or contact the Department of Building and Housing. One of the most important things to be aware of is the right of the tenants to give just three weeks' notice of their intention to move out; this could throw a spanner in the works if you are still away when they decide to move on. You are also required to give them six weeks' notice when you wish to return to your home.

We were very lucky in that we had excellent tenants; they paid the rent on time and looked after our house as if it was their own. To reassure them we weren't planning on coming back unexpectedly, we e-mailed them on a regular basis, which also gave them the opportunity to let us know how things were going.

Take into account that the rent you receive in these circumstances will be considered income and is, therefore, taxable. However, any reasonable expenses you incur for house maintenance while you are away can be claimed against this income (perhaps this might be a good time to get your house painted). It would pay to check out these possibilities with an accountant well in advance.

Other options include finding a reliable house-sitter. This involves someone living in your home rent-free or for a small cost, and in return for this they undertake to maintain the house, keeping it tidy and secure and, perhaps, also caring for your pet/s and garden. If the house-sitter is not known to you, do insist on appropriate testimonials – and check them out well in advance.

House-swapping is another way to reduce travel costs and over recent years quite a few websites have sprung up that are dedicated to this option. Try www.homeforexchange.com and www.homelinkint.org, or just Google 'house swap'.

If simply locking the door and walking away appeals to you, then consider whether you need to do any of the following to ensure the security and maintenance of your home while you and your family are away.

- Stop all deliveries, e.g. milk and newspapers.
- Arrange through your local Post Office for your mail to be held for you, or arrange for a trusted relative or friend to open your mail and act on your behalf.
- Book a local contractor to mow the lawn. Similarly, arrange for someone to look after any house plants.
- Install a timer on a light and/or radio so it appears that someone is living there.
- Notify the local police of your absence.
- Leave a house key and trip itinerary with a trusted friend or neighbour.
- Empty the refrigerator/freezer in case of a power stoppage and unplug all appliances to reduce the risk of fire.
- If you don't already have one, consider installing a security/fire alarm system.
- Turn off the water heater.
- Move valuables to a safe place – off the property with a friend is better than under the mattress.
- Make a list of possessions that you have lent out to friends or family.
- Check with your insurance company on their policy regarding a home left unoccupied. Sometimes the policy will lapse after a given period of time where the house is empty.

General things to tidy up before you leave include:

- returning your library books
- cancelling subscriptions
- redirecting mail
- tagging your bags with contact details
- setting up autopayments for utility bills
- backing up computer files, and
- making yourself a big list of things still to do!

Visas and passports

Make sure all your passports are up to date and will remain valid throughout your trip, and be aware that children these days must have their own passports. If any of you are eligible for a second passport from another country, bear in mind the cost and time required to get it versus the potential advantages.

Plan well in advance for the visas you may need. Check with your travel agent or look on the Internet or an up-to-date travel guide to find out which countries require New Zealand citizens to have visas. While some countries will issue visas at the border, others require them to be obtained in advance. In some cases this can take months rather than weeks, so start planning for this as early as possible.

Once you have all the appropriate documentation, make photocopies, particularly of your passports, just in case they get lost or stolen.

We shared the responsibility of carrying passports between the two of us, i.e. each adult carried their own plus one of the children's, thereby minimising the chances of losing all of the passports in one go.

Insurance

Travel insurance is expensive, especially if you're planning to be away for some time. Consider buying coverage for serious illness, travel disruption, loss of possessions or disaster only, rather than total coverage. This will depend to some extent on where you plan to travel, but in the main, insurance is designed to cover worst-case scenarios rather than any little inconvenience. Read the fine print on the documentation carefully before committing and take time to consider your circumstances.

While on the subject of worst-case scenarios, check that your life insurance is up to date. You might also want to take the opportunity to update your respective wills. The prospect of either parent dying while the family is overseas is rather sobering but needs to be dealt with.

As our children were mildly nervous about the possibility of something happening to either or both of us while we were away, we sat down and talked the issue through with them. They felt a lot more confident after this. It is a good time to stop and consider ALL the possibilities and make suitable legal arrangements.

Consider vesting a trusted relative or friend with Power of Attorney over your affairs in case you are unable to take care of such things yourself. You will also probably need your designated trusted helper to open mail, check your credit card statements, move funds between accounts, and pay some bills for you.

It is also well worth letting your bank manager know of your plans so he/she can help you as much as possible.

Cash at the ready

In this day and age, credit cards are probably the best way of paying for things while you're away. Even the smallest towns in Europe and the UK have ATMs, which can be very useful should you arrive out of banking hours and need some cash. This is particularly applicable outside the larger towns and cities of southern France, Spain and Italy when most if not all businesses are closed between 1 and 4 pm. Avoid keeping all your cash in one place, e.g. one of you might carry some in a wallet while the other keeps the balance in a money belt or similar.

Although we took travellers cheques for emergencies, we didn't use them. However, the two credit cards we took were put to good use: we used one for withdrawing cash from ATM machines and the other for all our actual credit card purchases, e.g. accommodation, food and petrol. We kept the first one topped up (i.e. in credit), thus ensuring we didn't get charged an extra fee for taking cash out, and arranged an automatic payment from our cheque account to pay off the other card each month.

Health issues

Depending on which countries you will be travelling in, you may need to consult a doctor to check which, if any, vaccinations may be necessary or recommended. Generally, it's not necessary for travel in Europe and the UK. If, however, you are going to Asia, Indonesia, South America or Africa, there will be some strong vaccination recommendations or requirements before entry is allowed. As some vaccinations must be given up to eight weeks before travel starts, be sure to allow enough time. Travel guides, travel doctors, specialist travel medicine books and websites cover this topic as well.

Having one adult family member complete a short St Johns first aid course could be very useful, not just for your family but for other travellers in time of need. In any event, a small but comprehensive medical kit is a necessity (see Chapter 2). Be sure to include specific drugs and potions that you use regularly, including both prescribed and over the counter medications. Take as much as you can get on your prescription (as long as it will fit in limited baggage space) and consider wearing a Medic Alert bracelet if the circumstances warrant it. It won't always be easy or even possible to get what you might need at short notice in non-English-speaking countries. Brand names may be unfamiliar and the packaging is often different.

Be aware of the implications of travelling in and out of countries with medication in your baggage. If you have to carry syringes or needles, e.g. for insulin or adrenalin administration, carry with you a letter from your

GP that states your diagnosis and the drugs you require. This could avoid some hairy moments at border control. And remember that the quantity of medication in liquid form or otherwise which you are allowed to carry on board planes with you is severely limited these days.

The most common medical complaint suffered by young children while travelling is that of diarrhoea/vomiting and associated dehydration. You can reduce the risks by encouraging thorough hand-washing prior to eating and, of course, after visiting public toilets, and by consuming bottled water wherever possible. This is not always easy given that tap water is used for making ice cubes and mixing juices, as well as for rinsing salad vegetables.

Many travel advisors will recommend avoiding food from street vendors. There's such a thing as being too careful and you may well miss out on some delectable culinary treats at markets and similar places. Use your common sense – if it doesn't look fresh, then don't eat it! But keep a balance between paranoia and enjoyment.

Our food experiences at markets in particular were just too good to pass up so we generally took the attitude that after raising and feeding our kids over a period of years we had a pretty good idea of what would be risky and what was likely to be safe.

A final note for those of you with special dietary needs – the Internet is a marvellous source of information. You could also consider making connections with support groups in the various countries you intend to visit. Another useful tip is to create some pocket-sized translations of your particular medical condition in the appropriate language/s and have them laminated so they are easy to show in restaurants and cafes.

Pearl has coeliac disease and her diet therefore needs to be gluten-free. The Internet gave us the opportunity to source restaurants and shops that might offer gluten-free options. We found all the restaurants and cafes were happy to make an effort on our behalf; they always liked to make an effort to please the children anyway.

Breaking the news to your kids

'I'm not going!' Isaac

It is vital that you get the 'buy in' of your children because if they are not happy, you won't enjoy your trip. The earlier you present the idea of the family OE to your children, the more time they will have to get used to it. It is a lot to ask of your children to step outside of the world they know and leave all their friends behind, and they will need time to adjust to that idea. Accentuate the positive but make sure they have a realistic view of what will be involved. This subject is covered in more detail in Chapter 3.

Our friends the Imminks posted out 'homesick boxes' ahead of them containing a few treats from New Zealand such as some pineapple lumps and a special book or magazine. We wished we had thought of this – especially with regard to books, as Isaac is a voracious reader and was constantly short of material. It is also worth investing in a book of games for car journeys or quizzing your friends for favourite time-killers on their family trips. Try www.theaa.com/arewenearlythereyet/index.html

Making the most of the delicious treats you come across in other countries is one of the many joys of travelling.

(Above) Sfogliatelle *is a regional speciality of Naples consisting of a cream or custard centre with crisp, flaky pastry on the outside, sprinkled with icing sugar.*

(Right) Pastis de nata *from Portugal – baked custard tarts, sprinkled with icing sugar or cinnamon or both. Karen and I found we 'needed' at least three of these each a day.*

(Above) Italian men enjoy the newspaper and a cappuccino under a fresco, Sorrento. Spending time with your male friends and watching the world (and the women) go by is a favourite pastime throughout Europe.

If you accidentally leave something behind, don't worry – there are lots of exciting places to purchase replacements.

(Right) Preparing the essentials.

Chapter 2:
What to take

Everyone will have their own priorities in terms of items of personal importance, but included in this chapter is a list of things we consider essential to take with you on your travels. Once you've decided on what you will and won't need, undertake a trial pack in your luggage of choice (more on that in this chapter), then take it for a test run somewhere, e.g. on the bus, in the car or on a weekend away.

Obviously your mode of transport will determine to a large extent how much you can take. The time of year will also have a bearing in that travel during winter months will require heavier clothes. Bear in mind, too, that the further you stray off the tourist route, the lighter and more portable your belongings need to be. Young children will not be able to carry much, which also needs to be taken into account because you will have to carry it for them. If you have a bigger budget, you can carry less

2: What to take

and buy more, and you can make more use of taxis.

Well before you leave, check with the airline/s on which you've booked to find out their weight restrictions. This will avoid hefty excess baggage charges. Be aware they are not standard, e.g. some of the cheaper charter airlines operating out of the UK, such as EasyJet and RyanAir, have stricter weight restrictions than most other international carriers.

We used a car for two-thirds of our time away, which allowed us to carry extra luggage and food.

Kid stuff

Most children, if given the opportunity, will want to take as much as possible. But once you point out – depending on their age, of course – that they will have to carry extras in their backpacks, they will soon cut it down to a few essentials. Although this might involve a bit of discussion and negotiation over weight, size and priority, it can be a good lesson for children in terms of possessions and their relative importance. You can always remind them that their full collection of books and toys will be waiting for them on their return and they'll have lots of fun rediscovering them.

Our kids each took an MP3 player, some books, pens and a blank notebook. This was topped off, in Isaac's case, with a Gameboy and a small container of Lego; Pearl added a deck of cards and a collection of small dolls.

Access to good books in English for children (let alone adults) can be an ongoing problem because it's just not possible to carry a whole lot. Also, bookshops that sell appropriate material for kids are few and far between. That's when mailing yourselves 'homesick boxes' (see Chapter 1) can really work well. Failing this, check out op shops in English-speaking countries for cheap and cheerful books. Hostels in various countries often have an informal book exchange programme too.

Adult stuff

You will probably want to take at least one camera. These days digital technology cuts down on a lot of space previously taken up by rolls of spare film. However, digital cameras require accessories. We suggest taking a spare battery and then rotating them, keeping one fully charged at all times. Large-capacity (e.g. 1 gigabyte) compact flash memory cards are good to take too – when they are full you can download the files to either a portable hard drive (PHD) or burn them to CD (card to CD services are available in most places at a reasonable cost). You may wish to avoid plugging your camera or PHD into computers at Internet cafes because of the risk of a virus. Therefore, take a USB cable and card reader if you anticipate having the use of trusted friends' computers. Don't forget to test your equipment before you go.

As for e-mailing images home, it is not always simple when you are on the move. You need a trusted (i.e. virus-free) computer and software to resize photos – the smaller the file, the easier it is to e-mail. Consider using a service such as Ofoto (www.kodakgallery.com) to share your trip photos. Or you could join a travel blog site, e.g. STA Travel Blogs or MyTripJournal.com, where you can create your own travel website, usually at no cost, which allows you to share photos and stories. It is best to set this up before you leave home.

We took a selection of music CDs (no cases, just the disks in a wallet) for the odd occasions that we got to listen to them. We decided against taking an iPod because it was not possible to share with the rest of the family (except in the car) and they are thief magnets. And while a laptop would have been great for sending and receiving e-mail, playing games, watching DVDs and storing photos, we decided against it because of the extra weight and the attraction to thieves.

Walkie-talkies can be very useful when you want to split up the children for a bit of time apart but not lose track of each other in busy places. They were very useful in crowded market places and provided for a bit of James Bond-like fun. The downside is that they chew up batteries very quickly and have a limited range, but it's possible to get good use out of them in certain circumstances such as museums, galleries and markets.

People around us were usually amused by our 'roger that' and 'over and out' speak when we were using our walkie-talkies. Only once were we asked to put them away by guards, and this was for security reasons.

Taking a mobile phone makes good sense but they can be expensive to run, particularly if you are set up for global roaming. This allows you to call (or text – much cheaper) home, and some families would find this invaluable. Another option is to simply take the handset and purchase SIM cards from the countries you visit as and when you need them. A third option is to rent a handset from a local provider. You can check the cost involved on the Internet before you leave.

If you do take your own handset, be sure to pack a charger (an extra one in the event you rent or buy a car is another good tip). Programme your phone with emergency numbers and instruct the children on how to use the phone in case the need arises.

We had a mobile phone that we used only occasionally. We found the most convenient and economical solution was to purchase a phone card for use in the public phone booths of each country we visited.

The art of packing

Check out the website www.onebag.com/ for some hints on what to pack for your trip. Keep clothing as lightweight as possible and choose colours that go well together so you can mix and match effectively. Include a couple of accessories to dress yourself up for when the occasion arises, e.g. a smart scarf or a nice belt. You pretty much have to make your own choices here but following are some basic principles to get you started.

- Keep your clothing low maintenance. Choose clothes that don't need ironing and remember that darker colours won't show marks as easily. This is critical for the children as the probability of them spilling food is directly proportional to the whiteness of the garment. You don't want to be doing laundry every day.
- When deciding between fabrics, be aware that synthetics tend to retain odours and as such need more frequent laundering than natural fibres. That said, modern fleeces are of course very quick-drying – handy when you're on the move.
- While jeans are very useful and practical items of clothing, they can take a long time to dry.

Our incredibly handy travel clothes line performing to expectations inside a mobile home in Belgium.

- Consider the comfort level of the clothes you'll be taking with you and make sure they include loose trousers, non-scratchy jumpers, good footwear, etc. Ask yourself, 'Will I be happy wearing this for up to 24 hours at a time?'
- Be prepared to lower your standards. There may well be times when you won't be able to get to a laundromat, which will involve having to extract yet another wear out of that smelly T-shirt and less-than-fragrant socks.

From Karen's diary: 'We are all tired, smelly and hungry. Had a long shower and put back on stinky clothes. Went out looking for pizza.'
Martina Franca, Italy

Getting your washing done can become quite the time and money waster while you are on the road. If you're lucky, you'll occasionally come across some accommodation where there is a free washing machine available or where your hosts are happy for you to throw in a load. Don't

It's easy and inexpensive to pick up new clothes while you are travelling, particularly at 97% discount!

be shy about asking if you can do your washing because it is something that you will have to deal with every week at least, and if you can avoid using a laundromat it's money saved – and an annoying job made easy. Laundromat dryers can be a rip-off (they just don't get that warm) so be sure to purchase a travel clothes line which is generally very effective given sufficient time and space.

Pack at the top those items that you will need to get at first. This may sound obvious but if you arrive somewhere late and just need toothbrushes and pyjamas for the children, it's good to get them to tired, scratchy little people with the minimum of drama.

How you pack your bags will make a difference to how much you can fit in. It is important that children learn to fold clothes instead of using the stuff-it-in approach that they do so well – you might find you have to pack for them otherwise. www.onebag.com has some good discussions on rolling up clothes versus folding them.

On average, we moved every 2–3 days so packing – and last-minute searches for overlooked items – became part of our routine, just like brushing teeth. Even so, kids are particularly good at losing things, so do remember to check under beds, under sheets, in the shower, etc. as you leave your accommodation. The same principle applies when you get off a train or bus.

If you're going to be away for any significant length of time, the children will almost certainly grow out of their clothes – you could plan for this and send new things on ahead of you, but it is much more fun to buy what you need when you need it. Throughout Europe and the UK you'll come across markets where clothing is really cheap, and making a purchase is great for your foreign language practice.

Comfortable footwear is vitally important for every member of the family. Don't cut corners and buy shoes at the last minute – you need to give everyone a chance to wear their shoes in and get used to them. It is worth spending money on good footwear given the amount of walking you're likely to do.

Consider your wardrobe in the light of different cultures and dress accordingly. OK, this is not compulsory but a word on cultural safety won't go amiss. In many countries it's expected that women will cover up when entering a mosque, monastery, temple or other place of worship. At the very least you can expect to cover your head and shoulders with a scarf or sarong. For this reason, you might want to take your own scarf for this purpose rather than use one that hundreds of other tourists have used earlier in the day.

During our travels, we saw young women enter churches and walk past the priest, with cleavages heaving in bikini tops (the women, not the priests) and/or very short skirts, and felt quite uncomfortable about this. Do respect the cultural 'rules' – it's just good manners.

Children are generally exempt from these rules but we encouraged our kids to follow the correct protocol so that they would understand more about other cultures.

> *From Pearl's journal: 'Today we caught the tram to the Blue Mosque where I had to wear some silly clothes.'*
> *Istanbul, Turkey*

Wardrobe basics

Consider the range of temperatures you're likely to encounter and pack accordingly (in our case we experienced temperatures ranging from –2°C to 42°C). A list of what we consider to be essential for each member of the family follows:

- 2 pairs woollen socks
- 2 pairs cotton socks
- at least 5 pairs of underwear (take extra for small children who could get caught short)

Don't forget those sleeping bags – you never know when you'll need them. Getting some sleep on the ferry from Corfu to Brindisi.

- 2 pairs of shorts
- 2 pairs of trousers (or a pair of zip-offs which can be either short or long)
- 3 T-shirts
- 1 dress shirt or dress/skirt
- scarf and/or sarong
- sleepwear
- 1 warm but light layer such as a sweatshirt or long-sleeved T-shirt
- 1 woollen jersey or polar fleece

- 1 raincoat
- 1 set thermal underwear (i.e. polypropylene shirt and longjohns)
- swimwear
- 1 woollen beanie
- 1 summer hat/cap

Karen: Especially for the women – after a few months in the same dowdy brown shorts and grey T-shirt, you may feel the need to be a little more feminine in your appearance. I carried a tiny box with jewellery (nothing too precious), a scarf which could double as a belt, a very small amount of makeup (mascara and lipgloss to be precise), a bottle of nail polish and a few hairclips. Of course, if you don't take them, there's always shopping!

Other stuff

There are any number of specialised travel shops or camping outlets waiting to take your money in exchange for lightweight, compact gear. But remember – you get what you pay for so it's probably prudent to buy items of reasonable quality in order to avoid having to replace them later. Shop around for bargains at outlet stores and sales. Here is a list to which you can add – or subtract – depending on your circumstances.

- Sleeping bags: if you plan to camp, stay in a mobile home or hostel-type accommodation then you'll need a sleeping bag. If the budget allows, opt for those which are compact and lightweight, but warm (or cool) enough to be suitable for the climate. Smaller-size sleeping bags can be purchased for young children.
- Cutlery set for each person. We chose a knife/fork/spoon set each that was secured by a split ring.
- Universal sink stopper (not all hostels provide a plug for the basin).
- Small backpack or shoulder bag for each member of the family for use on day-to-day outings.
- One pocket knife per adult.

- Travel clothes line (effectively two pieces of elastic cord twisted around each other and secured by a hook at each end).
- Spare batteries (yes, they're easy to buy but not always when you need them).
- Small sewing kit for minor repairs and lost buttons.
- A small multi-tool or similar (in case you need pliers, saw, screwdriver, etc.).
- A set of power adaptors that can be used in a variety of countries.
- Inflatable pillows (useful on long plane, train, bus and car journeys).
- Matches or a cigarette lighter. You never know when you need to set fire to something – candles, BBQs, exotic foreign cigarettes.
- Money belt for each adult. Particularly useful during air travel, train travel and other prolonged transits where there is the potential for thieves to ruin your day.
- First aid kit (see next section).
- Small, absorbent travel towels – plus we would recommend at least one beach towel between two people.

Souvenirs galore await you out there, and a hat for every part of your body.

- Toilet paper or box of tissues.
- Alarm clock or a wristwatch with an alarm.
- Torch and compass.
- A few small ziplock plastic bags.
- One or two small padlocks.
- And, as previously discussed, walkie-talkies, favourite music CDs, plus guide books and maps, toiletry bag and a small mirror.

Remember to keep knives, lighters, etc. in the main luggage, rather than your daypack or shoulder bag, to avoid embarrassing moments at airports.

I lost my cherished, twice-around-the-world pocket knife on one occasion – and the knife from my cutlery set on another – during a standard airline security check because I forgot to transfer it from my daypack to my suitcase before taking the former onto the plane!

A basic first aid kit

Needs will vary, but the following list should make a useful starting point.

- Personal prescription medications in the correct doses for adult and/ or child.
- Topical antibiotic cream.
- Paracetamol in the form your family usually uses, e.g. tablets for adults and syrup for young children.
- Ibuprofen syrup for fevers that don't respond to paracetamol.
- Antihistamine cream or syrup in case of allergy.
- Anti-inflammatory cream such as Voltaren, arnica or tiger balm.
- Anti-worm medication (children can easily pick up parasites from animals).
- Tea tree oil (acts as a fungicide, germicide and decongestant).

- Broad-spectrum antibiotic in case of infections (you will need to get this on prescription from your GP before you go, and write down the instructions for use).
- Gastroenteritis medicine.
- Sticking plasters – various shapes and sizes.
- Small sterile dressings.
- Sticking tape.
- Waterproof dressings.
- Steristrips.
- Length of gauze bandage (at least 5 cm in width).
- Thermometer, preferably digital rather than mercury for durability and ease of use.

Documentation

While you don't want to be weighed down with too much paperwork, it's a good idea to take photocopies of important documents including:

- relevant pages of your passport
- insurance information (particularly if you are planning on renting or buying a car)
- driver's licence (local and international)
- copies of birth certificates, and
- copies of receipts of any pre-purchased expensive items in case of theft, and of any other documents that would be inconvenient to lose. (Don't forget to make an extra copy of these items to leave with whoever is looking after your affairs at home.)

We also recommend printing out details of any pre-booked accommodation, particularly the address and phone number.

Luggage

Suitcases with wheels or backpacks – that is the question. If you choose the latter option you may find that sourcing a backpack to fit a small child can be a challenge – a daypack will probably be the best solution. Both options have their pros and cons, e.g. while suitcases are comparatively easy to get in and out of cars, planes, trains and buses, as well as being practical to wheel any distance (except in some of Europe's historic centres with narrow alleys and lots of steps), backpacks will go anywhere, no matter what the terrain, and they will stay with you when you get on or off transport – no getting stuck in ruts or cracks and flipping over.

If you think that most of your travel will be in cities and paved towns, then the wheelie suitcase might be the way to go. If you're going to be going 'off-road' a lot, then the backpack might still be the best option.

We chose to travel with backpacks, spending quite a bit of time on choosing them and subsequently trying them out. We found them to be excellent and they lasted the distance very well. In making the choice, it must have been the long-instilled tradition of backpacking in New Zealand that resulted in us not even considering 'wheelie' suitcases.

Whatever you choose, it's worth investing in good-quality products. Imagine how frustrating it could be if the wheels literally fell off your suitcase while you were some distance from your destination!

The markets in Europe offer fantastic food and wonderful visual experiences. (Above) Chickens for sale in Porto, Portugal, and (below) a dried fruit stall in Barcelona, Spain.

For apartment dwellers in Amalfi (above and right) and San Sebastian (below), space to dry the washing is at a premium.

The children enjoyed our visits to museums, galleries and famous sites all the more if they got an audio guide. Some venues have guides specifically for children.

(Right) Education on the road can be as simple as keeping up your reading.

Chapter 3:
What to do about school

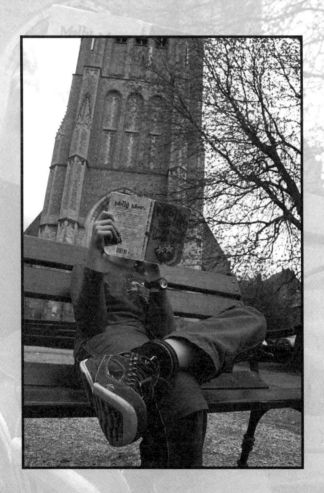

Plenty of people had something to say to us when they heard we were going away as a family. The comments we heard most included: 'You must be rich', 'Sounds great', 'Pity you have to take the kids', and 'What about school?'

Be prepared for a barrage of unsolicited comments and advice about the perceived wisdom of taking your children out of school for an extended time. How you choose to handle this is up to you, but be aware that you must advise the school of your plans and this should be done in writing. On receipt of your letter to the school, your child/children will be granted a three-month 'leave of absence' during which time the school can retain the funding for them. However, if you are going to be away for longer, your child/children will be removed from the roll, which means the school will lose the relevant funding. On your return, you will have to go through the enrolment process again. It might be that your children have a hard-fought-for place in the school because of zoning or other restrictions, in which case you will need to talk to the principal to do whatever you can to make sure their place is not lost.

When considering the timing of your trip, bear in mind the age and ability of your children. Consider whether the trip will interfere with formal exams and qualifications.

Home schooling

While it is possible to organise formal home schooling for the duration of your trip, it will require a lot of planning to allow for the ordering of relevant books and materials, mail pick-ups and drop-offs, perhaps a laptop computer, not to mention ensuring there'll be time and a place for the children to study whenever you stop along the way. All in all, we decided against it and opted for the 'absorption' method whereby the children would learn more from being immersed in new cultures, languages and histories, not to mention the physical and mental challenges of overseas travel. This decision was reinforced by their teachers who were both adamant that our children were likely to learn far more from travelling than they would at school. They were also quite certain that they would have no trouble catching up in the following year.

On his return to school, Isaac was given a list of a dozen cities to locate in Europe and was gratified to find he had visited 10 of them and so knew exactly where to find them on the map. Pearl was similarly gratified when she had the opportunity in her art class to discuss her self-portrait in comparison to the cubism of Picasso and the surrealism of Dali. She also chose to do a research project on Antoni Gaudi, having been impressed with his architecture in Barcelona. This is not something we mention to show off – it's simply that these things are now part of their real world and have meaning for them.

Although your children may not be doing formal schoolwork while you are away, don't ignore the chance to educate them en route. Each day will bring opportunities to introduce maths, science, history and so on. For example, converting currency is a good exercise in maths, as

Our 'flight' on the London Eye was more than just a holiday outing – we covered history, geography and maths, all in one go.

are sums involving time, distance and petrol consumption should you happen to be driving. Then there's all that art, history, geography and language to which they'll be exposed. Take the time to question them on things they have seen and done. Ask open-ended questions to challenge them to formulate their own opinions and ideas. And if they answer you with a question, throw it back at them, e.g. 'Why do *you* think that happened?'

They will also gain a good education in life skills such as problem solving, interacting with others, navigating, etc. You'll find your children spouting words in foreign languages and discussing the relative merits of Roman ruins, or pondering the implications of poverty and prostitution in big cities. The cool part is that the kids still see it as a holiday, not education.

We told our hosts, and any people who enquired about the children's education, that they were the educators while our children were travelling so it was up to them to make sure our children went home enlightened. A few people took this literally and went to the trouble of making themselves 'teacher' for the day and in the process provided unique learning opportunities.

Don't underestimate the power of osmosis. Children will take all sorts of knowledge on board without realising it and you will be amazed at how much general knowledge they retain.

Some children like a list of questions or a similar activity to work with during their visit to a gallery or museum. You can make these up in advance, getting information from guide books or websites, and then set the children up with paper and coloured pencils during the visit. Or you can do it on a more casual basis, i.e. asking questions as you go and perhaps afterwards to help reinforce the experience. This is a useful exercise at museums and galleries when the displays are too static. You can improve the interactivity by setting 'treasure hunts' to find particular objects. Every now and then, you will find a museum or gallery that already has worksheets set up for kids, such as the brilliant National Maritime Museum in Greenwich, London.

The ruins at Conimbriga contained fabulous examples of mosaic floors, going back to 200BC. Isaac's observation was that 'Quite frankly, there's not enough history for me'. But what he meant was that there was not enough written information provided at the site.

Beyond school

Be prepared to deal with uncomfortable topics as they arise. You'll almost certainly come across instances of poverty, prostitution and drug- or alcohol-related problems on a fairly regular basis – and that's just in the streets! When you visit museums and art galleries your children will be exposed to art depicting nudity, sex, torture and so on. You need to decide in advance how you'll handle the questions that are likely to be forthcoming from young and curious minds.

One of the galleries we visited in Europe featured The Rape of the Sabine Women, *the famous artwork by Rubens. Pearl, eight years old at the time, wanted to know what rape meant. We gave her an honest answer on this occasion and others, but without including unnecessary detail. She was then able to understand the concept without feeling upset or threatened.*

If you choose to take your family out into the world, it seems counterproductive to close your eyes or ears to it when these sorts of challenges arise. Once again, this is dependent on the maturity of your children and your personal philosophy, but if it is your personal choice not to discuss these issues with your children then prepare some answers in advance, because you will be asked!

A late Friday night Metro trip to see the lights on the Moulin Rouge proved to be an eye-opener for our family as we were not aware that it was still a busy and colourful red-light area. We gave up trying to shield the children's eyes from the graphic photos outside the various clubs, but we didn't linger too long. Predictably, there were lots of questions from both children about sex workers, particularly from Pearl who wanted to know why women chose to work in this industry. 'These days, people think sex is a form of entertainment!' was her closing observation.

Wherever you go in Europe, you will expose your children to a wealth of religious input – it is unavoidable. Religious history is deeply embedded in the culture and architecture of each country. What we loved about this was the opportunity to nurture within our children a tolerance of different cultures and faith systems. We hoped our children would learn to carry this tolerance with them into their adult life.

From Karen's journal: 'Spent the morning looking over the Mesquita. After seeing Catholic church followed by Catholic church, we took the opportunity to discuss Islam with the kids.

Then, finding a Catholic chapel in the middle of the mosque, Pearl stated, "Whaddya know, it's ANOTHER Virgin Mary!"

Keeping a journal

Although your children may rebel against keeping a journal (ours did for the entirety of the trip!), it's worth persevering because it will become a treasured souvenir in years to come. Some children will be keen as mustard to write a record of their trip and maybe even more so if you can organise an online journal. Good luck with this one.

From Karen's journal: 'I am having trouble getting my dreadful children to write their journals. They are distracted and unenthused, and we will have to resort to bribery.'

There is great value in children keeping journals, not just so that they can remember what they did and where they went, but in the absence of formal schooling it maintains the discipline of writing, recall and homework.

As a parent, you can help to make it more fun by encouraging them to save memorabilia, e.g. ticket stubs from exciting places. A journal is also a good place for them to record addresses of those people, e.g. children met along the way, with whom they want to stay in touch.

'I hated writing a diary but it is good getting out the diaries now and looking back over what we were doing last year.' Pearl

Views of Paris; a city that we all loved so much, we went there three times.

(Left) The Eiffel Tower – what an icon. We went up, down and around it several times.

(Above and below) Lively and spontaneous entertainment can be discovered on the streets of Paris, here at the market on Avenue Richard Lenoir.

(Above) A family-oriented hotel based around an indoor water park – what a great idea. The kids raved about their stay at Great Wolf Lodge in Niagara, Canada.

(Right) One idea to introduce to your children is that it is OK to be lost sometimes.

Chapter 4:
Introducing the idea
to your children

Not all children respond well to changes in routine and in order for them to buy into the prospect of an extended holiday overseas you need to allow them plenty of time to absorb the idea. In most cases, the children have no framework within which to put the idea of a prolonged overseas adventure. It is natural for them to be initially reluctant. Children, just like adults, will want to know, 'What's in it for me?' So the earlier you start to introduce the idea, the better.

'This [idea] is too big to comprehend. It's massive!' Isaac

Tell them about friends and relatives you are planning to visit, particularly if any of those households include children of a compatible age. Then there's the temptation of speciality shopping, such as the chocolate shops in Belgium, 'all-you-can-eat' pizza in Italy, and Hamleys

Toy Store in London. Make up a list of all those things that will have special appeal to your children and keep them somewhere prominent (e.g. on the fridge or family noticeboard) where they'll be seen on a daily basis. Encourage the children to add to the list themselves.

We used 'dangly carrots' to get our kids on board with the idea; for example, the idea of months off school worked wonders, as did planting the seed for visits to places that feature large in children's imaginations: Disneyland, Legoland, the Eiffel Tower, the Colosseum, etc.

> 'I slept in 96 different beds but, after the first few weeks, I started to get used to it. I sometimes had to sleep in the same bed as Isaac.' Pearl

Involve children in the planning

To get children as involved as possible, pin up a large map of the part of the world you'll be visiting. As your plans come together, stick coloured pins on the countries and cities you have decided as a family you really want to see. Encourage the children to add pins whenever they think of somewhere they would like to visit. Emphasise that it is the planning stage and any place is up for potential inclusion in the itinerary.

It was such a satisfying feeling when our children asked us things like, 'When we get to Italy, can we see Pompeii?' and we were able to answer, 'Yes, we'll try', and actually mean it! It was like being able to give our children the world. We ticked off the destinations as we travelled, and took great satisfaction in being able to say, 'This is my pin' when we arrived at pre-selected favourites. The thrill of this applied equally to parents and children.

In the meantime, you could further motivate the children by getting them to research those places they want to visit and in the process drawing up specifics about what they want to see or do. Older children might enjoy turning this into a research project, e.g. making up charts of statistics and facts they find out for themselves.

The Internet is a wonderful visual tool for children and will greatly assist in getting them involved in the planning of the trip. Let them search websites that show where they might be going, and get them to help you choose places to stay. Google Earth in particular is a fun way to look at some of the places you intend to visit. Consider setting up a family travel website and keep it up to date throughout your travels. This is a great way to record your adventures for friends and family to see.

Taking the children shopping for travel-related items is another way to keep them involved and in the spirit of the trip. Although shopping with children is not always a pleasant experience, it's likely they'll become more and more enthused about the trip as time goes on, especially when you get their input into purchasing decisions wherever possible.

Dealing with upheaval

One of the hardest aspects of travelling that children have to come to terms with is missing their friends. OK, there will be ample distractions in store for them, but there is no avoiding the fact that they will most likely miss their friends dreadfully, and they will possibly see this as the most negative aspect of going on the adventure.

Encourage them to stay in touch via e-mail – most schools are set up with their own e-mail address and many classrooms even have their own website. Check with the teacher before you leave. And don't forget the old-fashioned way of staying in touch via letters and postcards.

This also applies to members of your extended family, such as grandparents and favourite aunties and uncles. Keep emphasising the fun in store for them as they send and receive letters, postcards and e-mails. It is also worth reminding them that their friends and relatives will be stuck at home with school, homework and so on, wishing they could be away on such an exciting adventure.

The prospect of visiting theme parks like Parc Astérix
(shown here) and Disneyland can really help keep the
children enthused about your trip.

Most importantly, remind them that these much-loved family members and friends will still be there when they get back and, again, there will be great fun in store in terms of recounting adventures, and showing off souvenirs and photos.

From Pearl's journal: 'I've been sticking photos [of friends and pets] in this travel diary because it is only 4 days till we go away. So it is getting really scary.'

In the spirit of emphasising the positive, don't forget to remind the children that the home comforts they will be missing out on will be balanced out by having the parents with them 24/7, rather than distracted by work and chores at home. The kids will also have all that time off school, rides on planes, visits to world-famous locations ...

It will pay to let older children in particular know that they're unlikely to have the luxury of their own bedroom while you're travelling. We compensated for this to some extent by telling our kids that instead of the same boring old space, they were going to have multiple bedrooms over the time we were away together.

The children also have to deal with leaving all their toys behind. They usually have at least one toy to which they are particularly attached, so allow some space for this in your luggage – that special teddy or ragged security blanket could prove to be a great comfort, especially to younger children.

Another wrench for children is the prospect of leaving their pets behind. Get them to help with finding foster homes for the pets while you're all away, but make sure you do this well ahead so that children, pets and the lucky recipients have plenty of time to adjust to the idea. Give the children a photo of their pet/s so that they can tuck it into their personal journal.

We were lucky to be able to distribute our three frogs, two cats and one budgie among close friends and family, and the children were relatively comfortable with the arrangements. On the day we left, well-meaning friends gave us a heartfelt send-off, which included bringing along our budgie to say farewell. This triggered floods of tears from both children, which lasted until we got to the airport.

Depending on the health and life spans of your pets, you may need to forewarn the kids about coming home to find some of their loved ones have departed this mortal coil. This can also be difficult (and potentially expensive if the vet is required) for the person(s) looking after your pet so bear this in mind when selecting an appropriate minder.

Some kind of day-to-day routine will be really important – even if it's as simple as always telling the children at the start of each day what you've got planned. For example, 'Today we are going to a cafe for breakfast, then we will walk to a gallery not too far away, and after that we will head back to our room for a rest.' Travelling without any routines will quickly lead to insecurity on the part of children if you fail to take control of the situation. Children need to know what is happening on a regular basis. (There's more on this in Chapter 7.)

Every morning, without fail, Isaac would ask, 'So what are we going to do today?'

Language barriers

Not understanding other languages can prove to be something of a challenge for the children.

On one of our visits to the markets in Paris, a French man attempted to converse with Pearl in English. 'I will rip your heart out,' he said, which not surprisingly frightened her until we figured out what he meant to say was 'You steal my heart away'.

The upside to this dilemma is that children usually begin to learn and use words in a new language fairly quickly. Just as you encourage your children to use the words 'please' and 'thank you' in their own language, encourage them to do the same using their new vocabulary.

We were surprised that, at the beginning of our trip, as we travelled through Belgium and France in spring, it was around six weeks before we ran into someone who spoke English as a first language. We didn't come across any children with whom our own could speak English for around two months. This is difficult for children because they are taking in a huge amount of experiences and information but they can really only communicate and discuss these with their siblings and parents. The children would sit down and start swapping stories with any adults we came across who could understand them.

From Karen's journal: 'This evening at a restaurant, and after just three days in France, I noticed Isaac now says "Merci" automatically.'

It is really worthwhile for the whole family to learn basic greetings and phrases – hello, thank you, etc. – in the languages you will be exposed to. Consider buying either a phrase book or a guidebook that includes basic phrases, especially if you are spending several weeks in one country.

Children are generally confident in trying out new words, even if they use them incorrectly or inappropriately, because they are less afraid of getting it wrong and quickly realise that people appreciate someone who tries. Children will also quickly recognise the written language (they can help you read road signs) and will always let you know which shop sells ice cream.

Karen discovered a foolproof and international way of locating the toilet in a cafe, bar or restaurant by simply standing around wearing a mildly lost expression. Without fail, a helpful waiter or guest would soon point her in the right direction. Try it: it works. You have to be a bit more forward about walking into any old cafe and using the toilet, whether you intend to drink/dine there or not. Necessity rules and this behaviour is generally well tolerated.

Tate Modern, London. Is it art? Well, the jury is still out on that one. Is it educational? Absolutely! Maths, physics, history and art all rolled up together in one very fast slide.

Experiencing exotic architecture is just one of the benefits your children will derive from this trip.

Spain offered many options, including (left) Gaudi's Casa Batlló in Barcelona, (below) the Salvador Dali museum in Figueres, and (right, top) the astounding Guggenheim Museum, Bilbao.

(Right, bottom) Falling into the spiral staircase at the Vatican Museum, Rome.

(Above) A gondola ride was something we decided we just couldn't afford despite it being a virtual 'must do' during a visit to Venice. This is the sort of decision you may face during your travels.

(Right) Our wonderful £450 car, Megalith.

Chapter 5:
Budget

From Isaac's journal: 'Daddy's having a stingy day.' Edinburgh

'How much will it cost?' is the question we have been asked more than any other, and no surprises there. It is the key to how comfortably you can travel, how far and for how long. There is, of course, no simple answer. There will be some fixed costs such as airline fares, but after that costs can vary enormously. Establishing a daily budget that covers accommodation, meals, incidental travel, sightseeing, etc. is a good idea if you need – like most of us – to keep costs under control.

The cost of our trip, for two adults and two children for a period of eight months, was just under NZ$75,000 in total, or NZ$9000–10,000 per month. It was our intention not to exceed NZ$200 (€100) per day and, even though that was not often possible, it was good financial discipline for us. Karen and I felt that to have been more frugal would have compromised the family's comfort and enjoyment.

It's not always easy to write down everything you spend, but keeping some kind of record will be useful to keep track of how well or how badly you are faring. It can also help you with on-the-spot decisions on whether to splurge on a meal out, for example, or conserve the money.

Once you've arrived in a part of the world where you'll be spending any length of time, you can break down the costs you'll incur into four main categories: accommodation, food, transport and sightseeing. As shopping is a category in its own right and as everyone will have different priorities, we're not going to include advice about this other than suggesting that if you want to purchase lots of goodies along the way, work it into your budget.

Transport

The idea of buying a second-hand car in which you can travel around will probably appeal to many people for obvious reasons. For those of you whose first stop will be the UK, check out www.autotrader.co.uk before you leave on your trip, or you can wait until you arrive and shop around the dealers or wade through the newspaper advertisements.

We bought a cheap car (£450), a Ford Mondeo station wagon, that turned out to be as reliable as we had heard they were supposed to be, but we did take the precaution of having it looked over by a mechanic before we actually bought it. It looked to us to be of similar shape, character and reliability as the rows of megalithic stones we saw in Carnac, France, so we named it Megalith – it never skipped a beat in the entire five months and approximately 15,000 km of motoring that we put it through. We chose to buy a right-hand drive car in England (and not a left-hander on the Continent) on the grounds that driving on the wrong side of the road might be easier if we at least felt comfortable with the controls. It also made sense to make this important purchase in a country where English was the first language.

You don't have to hold a passport for the country in which you buy a car, but you must have a valid driver's licence from your own country.

It is also recommended that you purchase an International Driving Permit (IDP) before you leave home. They cost around NZ$20 at the time of publication, are issued on the spot and are valid for 12 months.

Be prepared to pay a lot for petrol. You might think it's expensive here but it's *really* expensive over there (around twice the cost when we travelled in 2006, with diesel almost as costly). Check out www.aaroadwatch.ie/eupetrolprices/ for current costs in Europe, www.gasbody.com for the same in the USA and www.kshitij.com/research/petrol.shtml for world prices.

For those who do purchase or hire a car in the UK and then take it to Europe, be aware that the vehicle must display a GB sticker and you will need proof of insurance. You must also carry on board two warning triangles, two high visibility vests and have stick-on 'adjusters' for your headlights (which stop your 'left-hand-side-of-the-road-adjusted' headlights blinding on-coming traffic) – or risk being fined. All of these items can be easily sourced from a car parts retailer. A first aid kit is also highly recommended (see Chapter 2). In the event of an accident or breakdown, your insurance company will instruct you on what to do. If time allows, visit AA websites to check out the definitive source of information regarding overseas driving requirements.

People choose to drive rather than rely on public transport for many different reasons. Advantages include the ability to carry more luggage, and you can take your own food for lunches and snacks which keeps costs down. Driving also allows you to go where you want, when you want, without having to wait for buses, trains or other public transport. This also applies if your choice of wheels isn't confined to a car.

Campervans (think Kiwis in Kombis) are very popular, either as an outright purchase or hired for the duration (check www.autotrader.co.uk and www.ebay.co.uk). If you do buy one, the up-front expense for a campervan is much higher but you may recoup that and more in what you save on accommodation. Plus, you should be able to recoup some or all of your initial cost when you sell it later. Travelling like this will also allow you to carry larger items, e.g. bikes, surfboards or skis.

(Left) London, England. Twenty-five hours from Auckland and it shows on Isaac's face as, jet-lagged and slightly stunned, he negotiates our first Underground trip on Day 1.

(Below) History surrounds you in London. Getting interactive at the British Museum, Pearl handles a 2000-year-old Roman coin.

(Right) Lego, Lego everywhere ... A boy's own adventure in Hamleys Toy Store in London's Regent Street. The 'toy overload' will wow kids, as will the general West End buzz.

(Left) Bruges, Belgium. The first of many mobile homes that we sampled during our trip. They were a pleasant surprise in terms of space, comfort and affordability.

(Below) Paris, France. Enjoying a bit of 'down time' in our city apartment. It was small but affordable, and the central location was a bonus welcomed by all.

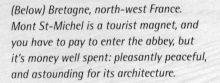

(Below) Bretagne, north-west France. Mont St-Michel is a tourist magnet, and you have to pay to enter the abbey, but it's money well spent: pleasantly peaceful, and astounding for its architecture.

(Background photo) Giant sand dunes – Arcachon, southern France.

(Above and right) Arcachon, near Bordeaux, south-west France. Grand Dune de Pyla is an experience for the active and the not so active. It's great family fun.

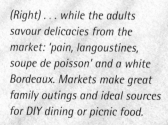

(Left) Paris, France. Isaac's idea of 'parfait' French cuisine is an entire crunchy baguette to himself . . .

(Right) . . . while the adults savour delicacies from the market: 'pain, langoustines, soupe de poisson' and a white Bordeaux. Markets make great family outings and ideal sources for DIY dining or picnic food.

(Above) Ribadesella, Spain. Language is no barrier to making friends.

(Right) The bullfights don't attract as many people as they used to but are still a big part of the cultural life of Seville. Both children found the spectacle disturbing and didn't want to stay long in the arena.

(Below) Santiago de Compostela, Spain. In continental Europe, being out and about at night is part of the fun. On our way to find dinner but stopping to pose in front of the magnificent Catedral del Apóstol.

(Background photo) Mosaic on Casa Batllo by Antoni Gaudí - Barcelona, Spain.

(Left) Seville, Spain. When the temperature hit 42°C, the kids jumped fully clothed into a fountain. Sometimes it's better to have a siesta during the sweltering midday heat.

(Below) Seville again. 'That's music to my mouth!' announces Pearl on treating herself to 'chocolate con churros' (doughnuts dunked in hot chocolate).

(Right) Barcelona, Spain. Las Ramblas street theatre delighted and entertained the children for the price of a few coins.

(Above) Lisbon, Portugal. The impressive 5000 cubic metre tank of the Oceánario keeps Pearl enthralled. The aquarium and its associated science park were a highlight for the children.

(Right) Sesimbra, Portugal. Preparing the (six only) sardines for the BBQ, a home-and-away tradition.

(Left) Porto, Portugal. Interactive water play/science, and a great time playing under fountains and jets of water at the Parque de Cidade.

(Above) Évora, Portugal. Foreign travel can broaden children's palates . . . even though Luke was the only family member brave enough to dine on the Portuguese delicacy of caracóis (snails).

(Right) Conimbriga. Walking among the ruins at Portugal's best-preserved Roman city, which dates back to the ninth century BC.

(Left) Braga, Portugal. The children surprised us by really enjoying the long hike uphill to visit the twelve stations of the cross and the zigzag stairway of Bom Jesus do Monte. A combination of religious experience and physical workout.

(Left and below) Snowdonia National Park, north Wales. Making new friends (Scousers Ron and Bobbi) on the road is a bonus to travelling, and an icy swim near the summit of Mt Snowdon makes the hot 10 km walk all worthwhile for Pearl.

(Background photo) Tartan scarves – Edinburgh, Scotland.

(Left) Stonehenge, south-west England. The extra cost of an audio commentary is worth it to both occupy and educate kids, providing you can listen without distractions.

(Right) Inverness, northern Scotland. A rare opportunity to handle real weapons at the tattoo thrilled both children.

(Below) Cardiff, south-west Wales. Meeting family members for the first time, like Welsh Uncle Gordon in his eccentric garden, provides fond memories.

(Below) Cornwall, England. A roadside exploration of mysterious standing stones provoked interesting discussions about ancient civilisations.

(Above) Istanbul, Turkey. Pearl wears culturally appropriate dress for our visit to the Blue Mosque, while . . .

(Right) . . . Isaac wanders the Grand Bazaar, intrigued by the many treasures and interesting characters.

(Background photo) Kilim – Cappadocia, Turkey.

(Left) Waiting at Istanbul for our overnight train to Ankara. Ten-thirty at night and it's still 35°C! The sleeper cabins were remarkably comfortable and we all enjoyed the adventure of spending the night on the train.

(Left) Uçhisar, Turkey. The House of Memories restaurant provided plenty of good memories for our family. Luke entertains on the Turkish saz – more hilarity than a musical experience.

(Above) Cappadocia, Turkey. The kids couldn't quite believe that people lived in these cave houses. A walk through the unique landscape of Pigeon Valley.

(Right) Çirali, Turkey. The chimera of Mt Olympos is a naturally combustible gas escaping from the rocks. Freedom to play with fire is something your parents almost never give you at home.

(Above) Athens, Greece. Ruins of colossal proportions at the Temple of Olympian Zeus give a sense of history and wonder, although Isaac's favourite memory is of the 'cute puppies' we saw there.

(Left) Navigating Europe's metro systems becomes second nature to the children. Here the race is on to work out the fastest route to the next platform in Athens.

(Right) Athens again. Pearl is inspired to catch up on quality drawing time at the Children's Art Museum.

(Background photo) Komboloi (worry beads) – Athens, Greece.

(Above) Rhodes, Greece. The kids have to carry their own gear in backpacks, this time within the old city walls.

(Right) Crete, Greece. A week at Loutro gave the family an idyllic 'anchor point' topped with Cretan hospitality.

(Below) Delphi, Greece. A peaceful and educational moment sketching the ruins.

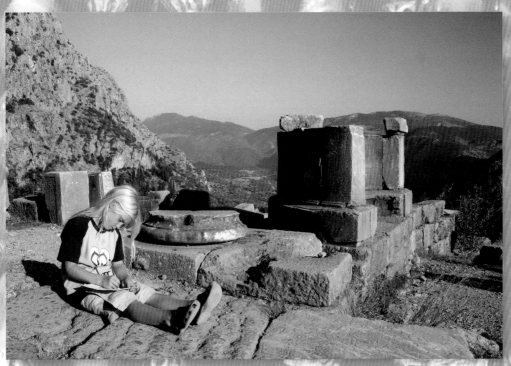

(Above) Rome, Italy. You have to get used to sharing the top tourist attractions, such as the Pantheon. We were 'lucky' because we only had to queue outside the Vatican Museum for 45 minutes.

(Left) Pearl tosses a coin into Rome's Trevi Fountain and makes the traditional wish. What you can't see is that the fountain is surrounded by tourists, 20-deep!

(Below) Vatican City. Pearl enjoyed this opportunity to write postcards to her friends at one of the world's most noteworthy post offices.

(Background photo) Carnival masks – Venice, Italy.

(Above) Pompeii, Italy. Crossing the road, Isaac walks where Romans went before him in the fourth century AD.

(Above) Sorrento, Italy. The vibrant colours and mouth-watering flavours of gelati never fail to appeal to kids.

(Left) Pisa, Italy. The markets offer fresh local produce that is hard to resist, and they also provide opportunities to meet locals.

(Above) Burlington, Ontario. Watching a friend play little league ice hockey.

(Left) Burlington again. In the woods north of Toronto, at below-zero temperatures. The park attendant we met was only wearing a light jacket and said he was 'looking forward to it getting cold'!

(Below) Niagara, Canadian border. The majestic falls are better seen if you can reach the telescope.

A campervan will suit some families well, but it can be an insular way of travelling in that it is harder to mix with locals when you are sleeping and eating under one roof as it were. Another possible disadvantage is that camping grounds tend to be on the outskirts of towns and cities, which can cramp your style if you want to be in the thick of things. Camping grounds are, however, a great place to meet other travellers.

We were both delighted and saddened to sell our mighty Megalith on www.ebay.co.uk for £310. That equated to five months' driving for £140 plus insurance of about £100 (and €10 for a flat tyre). All things considered, that was pretty good value.

If you go by car, then it is vital to sort out who's going to drive and who's going to navigate – and then accept those roles without arguing. It can be very stressful driving into big cities for the first time making it almost inevitable that you'll get a bit lost and end up going 'around the block' a few times. One-way streets are common and can catch you out.

> From Karen's journal: 'Drove into Bilbao today which quickly became a driver's nightmare. With me navigating and Luke tackling the peak-hour traffic, it took us about two hours to find and get to our YHA. Still, we held it together and didn't once get mad at each other. A big relationship test.'

You might want to consider investing in an electronic navigation device to avoid this problem; they're relatively cheap in Europe.

Another unexpected cost for private transport, which you will have to consider if you're planning to stay in apartments, is parking, especially in the larger cities. There are generally plenty of parking buildings available, but they're not cheap: it cost us €120 to park the car for a week in Paris. Ouch! On the plus side, they tend to be covered by CCTV surveillance.

Toll roads in Europe, especially in Spain and France, can be hard on the pocket. Although these roads can save time and ease the pain of long car journeys with children, the cost can sometimes outweigh the benefits of taking 'A' roads, i.e. lesser roads, which save money and afford you a better look at the countryside. It pays to find out in advance (visit www.theaa.com/allaboutcars/overseas/european_tolls_select.jsp) about toll roads so you don't get caught out. Then you can balance up the choice between fast and possibly picturesque.

We got nailed for tolls three times within the space of about five kilometres, going from south-west France into Spain, and copped €20 worth of tolls driving from the south of Spain to Barcelona. Our first toll gate threw us completely. You drive up to a machine and take a ticket stamped with a record of where you entered the toll road. When you leave the toll road, you pass a booth and pay the due fee for the distance. (Incidentally, it helps having the toll booth on the passenger's side of a right-hand-drive car, as it allows the navigator to deal with the cash, leaving the driver free to focus on the road.)

Flustered by toll gates, we got caught out a couple of times by forks in the road, straight after the booth, that allowed drivers to go one way or the other along the toll road, e.g. south or north. There was a mad scramble for the map as we tried to remember which way we needed to go, but after a few such run-ins we got used to it.

Renault and Peugeot both offer great new car leasing options within Europe, which are best value in the one-to-six weeks range. Check their respective websites or ask your travel agent for details.

We found that in a number of countries road signs announced major directions well before an intersection, but as we got closer to the turn the directions would disappear and be replaced by signs for local villages, some of which were too small to feature on our map. We eventually learnt to remember the major road signs. And while we're on the subject, here's another navigational tip: town centres are usually indicated by a black and white sign of concentric circles – very useful if that's where you want to get to.

Public transport

If you're not going to buy a car or campervan, then public transport is an affordable way to get around the UK and Europe. To find out the vast range of options on offer, e.g. bus, train, ferry, etc., then once again the Internet is your best friend, ably supported by various travel guides such as those in the Lonely Planet range. You'll find plenty of Internet cafes en route at which you can easily get online for prices and destinations.

Consider rail passes or bus passes that offer concessions, such as a family pass. It can be much cheaper than buying individual tickets, especially when the pass is for a day or longer – very useful if you're planning on undertaking a number of different sightseeing trips.

When we were in Venice, we bought a €100 (ouch!) family pass that allowed us 72 hours of unlimited vaporetto and bus rides. Not only was it much cheaper than individual fares, but more importantly it allowed us to jump on and off without the inconvenience and anxiety of having to pull out a wallet and pay each time.

Not all countries offer children's fares. And among those that do, not only does the qualifying age differ from country to country, but each form of transportation may have its own rules, e.g. most bus rides in Italy were free for children but train fares tended to be at full price for children over four years old. Ticket sellers generally rely on your honesty with regards to purchasing children's fares and seldom ask for proof. In general, children under 12 get cheaper fares but there are many exceptions. The other thing to bear in mind is that children's fares are not always clearly advertised so when in doubt, always ask. Again, check the Internet before you leave for up-to-date information.

Eurorail, which offers unlimited train travel between as many as 18 countries or can be purchased specific to one country, is probably the best known rail pass in Europe, but there are plenty of others – see your old friend the Internet again (www.ricksteves.com has useful advice on rail passes around Europe). Youth passes are available for 12- to 26-year-olds on some lines. Train travel is less flexible than having your own vehicle; you may experience delays which lead to grizzly children, and it drops you in the hangout zone of pickpockets. Generally speaking, travel has to be undertaken on consecutive days, which will require a bit of planning in advance. Also worth knowing is that some rail or bus passes can be combined with rental car deals while others include ferry travel. In many cases reservations are not required and so precious time (and grizzles) is saved. Trains are generally a safe mode of travel, and you can look out the window, watch the countryside without the hassle of driving and let the noise of the tracks lull you to sleep. Kids can stretch their legs and thus avoid going stir-crazy, and you don't have to make endless toilet stops. Overnight trains can be exciting, comfortable and save on accommodation costs. All in all, there's a lot of great things about train travel and they can be a very economical way to travel.

By the way, when catching a train in Italy, you must remember to validate your tickets at a machine for the purpose located on the platform before getting on. The alternative is risking the wrath of the conductors – they can be scary!

On one memorable Paris Metro ride, a blind man got on with his white cane to beg from the passengers. The children had learnt that if a blind person can't hear you they might not detect you are in your seat, so they became very quiet (an unusual event in itself) and tried not to giggle. Then a second blind man with white cane entered at the opposite end of the carriage. When each man recognised the presence of the other, there ensued a white cane blind man fight, each swishing his cane at the other and using some fruity French language. At this point, the children could contain themselves no longer and, having given away their location, would probably have been the next target for a good caning had the two men not been thrown off at the next stop.

Accommodation

Families travelling on a budget have a wide variety of accommodation options to choose from: Youth Hostels, independent hostels, pensions, apartments, bed and breakfast places, camping grounds and budget hotels. There are some other less-frequented options such as language schools, convents and monasteries, private homes, time shares, and Servas (a network of hosts organised by the Servas International peace movement – for details, see http://joomla.servas.org/).

We compromised on price, space and location, but we tried always to choose somewhere that was safe and sufficiently comfortable for the children to be happy – because, as every parent knows, if the children are unhappy, the parents will be unhappy.

Ribadesella, Spain. Just one of the amazing pensions that we stayed in. The rooms were only adequate but it is situated right next to the beach and has beautiful views.

You've got to look after your children if you want them to stick with you for this wild adventure. Mostly, we went for places with kitchen facilities and, wherever possible, our own bathroom. We did also opt for a TV when the opportunity arose (shame!) because it was a bonus for the children, and we could always justify it as a foreign language educational opportunity. Ha!

You can't always get it right. We booked our accommodation in Lisbon through a website before we left New Zealand. On our arrival we were delighted with our choice: the parking was great, the rooms were wonderful and the establishment had a real charm about it with its antique furniture, creaking staircases and crucifixes above the beds. The drawback was that it was located right in the middle of the city's drug and prostitution centre. We didn't realise this until we went for our first night-time walk when we quickly noticed the distinct change in character from the daytime. On checking our travel guide, we discovered we were in a 'no-go' area after dark and that the Metro station outside always closed by 9 pm because it was too dangerous thereafter.

As it happened, we stuck close to each other, kept to the well-lit streets and none of us came to any harm – and it provided a good opportunity for family discussions about drug use and prostitution.

After security and comfort, our next-most important criterion was cost. We tried to keep our accommodation cost to around €50–60 per day, which was manageable in France and Greece, easy in Portugal, Spain and Turkey, but impossible in Italy (where €100 per day is common), and tough in the UK (where €60–90 was the norm).

After a series of squeaky and uncomfortable beds, with springs so hard they left a dent in my hip, not to mention hostels with rattling aircon systems or rowdy neighbouring bars, we finally formulated a strategy for checking out accommodation prior to committing to stay and pay. We had quickly learned that once you've all lugged your packs up six flights of stairs, it's hard to say 'no' to a room so one of us would go with the host while the other stayed with the bags. Then the one who'd

seen the room and checked out the comfort and noise levels would give a brief but
very fast report (this in an attempt to discuss it in front of the host without giving
offence) to the other, e.g. 'bedOKbithardnotmuchspacebutitwilldo', and a decision
would be made.

Youth Hostel Association membership can be invaluable; membership
cost is modest and allows access to over 40,000 hostels worldwide plus
travel discounts. New Zealand children aged under 18 can join at no
cost. It's best to allow at least two weeks prior to departure to receive your
membership cards but some outlets, e.g. the iSite at Auckland airport,
will issue them on the spot. Hostel costs vary from country to country
as does the quality of hostel buildings and facilities. Those in France and
the UK tend to be well-run, well-equipped, comfortable and in good
locations, whereas those in Portugal are less attractive. (However, lower
prices in Portugal mean resorts and hotels may be within your budget.)
In general, though, hostels are a family-friendly source of adequate
and inexpensive accommodation. Staff members attempt to keep you
together and give you priority for rooms with private bathrooms. Some
hostels even have family rooms. Staff are also usually happy to make
ongoing bookings for you. And as the shut-out times and curfews of
yesteryear are in most cases no longer enforced, you can come and go as
you please, and that's important when your children need an afternoon
snack or rest.

Very few, if any, hostels in Spain and Portugal have kitchens because
eating out is so cheap. Also, youth hostels are not generally located in
the thick of things so they become a more attractive option if you're
travelling by car rather than public transport. However, many are based
in interesting buildings, so you may get to stay in a sixteenth-century
castle or the old fish works at the end of a wharf.

YHA costs for our family of four varied from €26 in Braga, Portugal, to £70
(€105 – ooof!) in Edinburgh, Scotland.

There is also a network of independent hostels throughout Europe and these are an excellent option too. They provide equally useful accommodation at competitive prices (check out www.hostelworld.com, www.hostelbookers.com and www.hostels.net). A phone call ahead is all that is generally needed, but you can book online without extra fees and membership is not required.

Feature cities like Paris, Rome, London and Barcelona will cost you a lot more but there are bargains to be found, especially via the Internet. Pensions, private apartments and hotels are readily available (check www.holiday-rentals.co.uk and www.ownersdirect.co.uk). Apartments are a good, economical option for families and provide some sense of normality with their vague resemblance to an actual home. A private apartment has the added bonus of being available during the winter season when lots of pensions and hostels are closed. Note, though, that most accommodation still works on multiples of two, e.g. doubles, twins and family rooms for four. If you are travelling with three or more kids, better to leave some at home. Just kidding! You may need to track down family rooms that can manage an extra bed.

We decided that there was no point in going to Venice unless we had a nice central place to stay. That meant paying big bucks. After hunting for ages on the Internet, we finally found a small but perfect apartment for €140 per night, with a helpful host and a wonderful rooftop garden overlooking the canals.

Camping grounds are another budget option, and you don't have to have a tent or campervan because many of them offer caravans or mobile homes – and cottages in some cases – for short-term stays. Advantages include a bit of peace and quiet, the opportunity to meet fellow travellers including other families, and the chance to cook your meals yourselves, thus saving some money. Generally, though, they do not provide bedding so you will need to have your own sleeping bags and linen, and they usually shut down altogether out of season.

Camping grounds in Europe are very different to the ones we were used to in New Zealand. Some of them are vast and include restaurants, theatres, pools, hydroslides and various other forms of entertainment. They often belong to a chain of branded or affiliated camping facilities; we picked up a map for one company that operated over 100 camping grounds in France alone. Camping grounds tend to be open only for holiday periods but offer great bargains during shoulder seasons.

Food and drink

It is important to remember that in many countries in Europe culture, climate and food go hand in hand. In order to enjoy a country and soak up its true essence, you need to stroll the avenues, take a drink at an outdoor cafe, eat late and dawdle over your food. Avoiding eating out in order to save money isn't always the best option in terms of a memorable cultural experience for your family. For many Europeans, food is more than just a necessity; the anticipation, the preparation and the enjoyment of it is part and parcel of their lifestyle – and it's surely this, among other things, that you have come to experience.

> From Karen's journal: 'Ordered up a feast in a Spanish bodega, fresh anchovies and la Mancha cheese with red peppers, chorizo cooked in cider, and as requested by Isaac, a large plate of grilled baby cuttlefish, barbecued with salt and lemon. Isaac tried the baby cuttlefish and didn't much like it, but we thought that it was the best dish we'd had so far.'

You'll find that between countries there is a big difference in the cost of food and drinks, whether it's from the local supermarket or in a cafe/restaurant. In parts of southern Europe you don't need to spend much to be able to enjoy a drink or two on a deliciously humid evening in an outdoor cafe, while the cost of a similar scenario in Paris, for example, may well take your breath away. It is helpful to know that in a French cafe, coffee is half the price if you stand up at the bar to drink it.

Karen and I loved the food in Spain and greatly enjoyed the experience of eating out most nights for around €25-35 for the family. Prices were similar in Portugal and Greece, and a little cheaper in Turkey (around €20-30). A basic meal for the family increased to more like €40-50 in France and €50-60 in the UK.

When self-catering is not an option and you need a cheap meal, fast food is hard to beat. In Greece, we were able to fill up the whole family on gyros pita for around €15, often including a drink each. And as for drinks, you can purchase perfectly quaffable wine in the supermarkets of most European countries for around €2–3 a bottle (although you can also find plenty that is worth pouring down the sink at this price as well). A six-pack of beer from the supermarket in France is about €3–4 and a casual drink with your friends in a public place, such as the park or beside a canal, is very acceptable behaviour.

From Karen's journal: 'Took advantage of the Granada custom of free tapas with every drink. Nice big portions. Buy 3 beers and dinner is taken care of as well.'

Eating out over a period of time can become tedious, which is where the advantages of self-catering accommodation become attractively apparent. It can be cheaper, too, not to mention a wonderful opportunity to visit local markets for local delicacies such as cheeses and salamis, wines, bread and olives, all of which are ideal snack and picnic foods too. They're a great way to practise the language, too. In order to give yourself a bit of browsing time, give the kids a couple of Euro to spend as they wish.

From Pearl's journal: 'We went to the spice market and I bought some Turkish delight and Isaac bought some nuts. Everyone pinched my cheeks and touched my hair.'

Supermarkets sometimes form a pleasant respite from the mentally draining exercise of using an unfamiliar second language. You can take time to look at what's on offer, get around at your own pace, and when it's time to pay you only have to provide a smile when you're handed the till docket. This can be blessed relief when everyone is tired and you just need to grab some supplies and get out again.

In many European supermarkets, you have to weigh your fruit and veges before you get to the checkout. The scales have pictures on them of the appropriate item, you press the button and out pops a sticker with the weight and price. We held up a few checkout queues before we worked this out. Be warned ...

Istanbul, Turkey. One of the many charming and colourful ice cream merchants who were so friendly to the children.

Children need to eat often and they often need to eat NOW! It is important to plan your food requirements because stopping for emergency supplies on a regular basis can become expensive. If you're travelling by car, you'll have space to carry extra food. Some kind of cooler bag in which you can keep perishables such as cheese, salami and milk is highly recommended. This is also worth maintaining on a small scale if you are backpacking.

Both our kids adore ice cream and took every opportunity to enjoy their favourite treat wherever they could. Ice cream is great for cooling down hot little bodies in summer, it gives them a boost of energy, it's relatively inexpensive and, especially important for Pearl, most is gluten-free. During our travels we used it as a treat, a destination, a social experience and, on occasion, as a bribe. Quite early on the kids figured out how to ask for an ice cream in Spanish, French, Italian, Turkish and

Greek, respectively, so it was kind of an educational experience as well. The kids were escorted through restaurants many times by proud and friendly owners to choose desserts that included their old favourite.

Sightseeing

Sightseeing can be an expensive exercise when you travel as a family and needs to be factored into your budget accordingly. It is possible to research the relevant costs through the Internet ahead of time so you've got a fair idea of what you are going to be in for.

In the UK, check out websites such as www.lastminute.com for special deals on parks, attractions and shows (this site also offers deals on accommodation and travel). The savings can be huge.

Prepare yourself and your children for the fact that it won't be possible to do or see everything, which means that sometimes you will have to say 'no'. Children will also have different priorities and will be very put out if you consistently pay for entry to museums but not for water parks or theme parks. An advantage to travelling with older children is that they can sometimes do activities or visit sites without you.

When we went to see the Leaning Tower of Pisa in Italy, the cost per head was €15 – no family pass or children's discount – so Karen went up with the kids while I enjoyed a peaceful coffee down below. The €15 we saved covered the cost of dinner for the children that night.

Ideally your budget should be able to cover the occasional 'must see' sight or activity that you had not counted on. Our advice is to pay up, enjoy it and accept it as part of the fickle fun of family travel.

We happened to be in Inverness at the time of the annual Military Tattoo and although we had not budgeted for it, we made an impromptu decision to go, and just as well – it was a fabulous show, delightfully Scottish and, best of all, not hugely expensive. In the beautiful Portuguese town of Sintra we found the Palacio Nacional

All of the national museums in Wales were free, including this, the wonderful National Slate Museum at Llanberis. The name doesn't inspire confidence but the kids loved it. The man in the photo is giving a demonstration of how to cut a slate tile. Isaac was thrilled when he was allowed to turn off the giant water wheel at the end of the day.

de Sintra closed (despite our travel guide saying it would be open that day) but we went on, reluctantly in my case, to the Palacio Nacional da Pena, which was an absolute gem! It's a fairy-tale castle on a mountain ridge overlooking Sintra and Lisbon, and we all adored it. You just never know.

If you enjoy visiting historic homes and beautiful gardens and you're going to be spending some time in the UK, it's well worth joining the QEII National Trust of New Zealand or the New Zealand Historic Places Trust. Membership of these organisations gives you free or concessionary admission, plus free parking, at all of the National Trust sights in England, Scotland and Wales, and other countries that hold a reciprocal agreement with New Zealand, including Japan, Australia and Zimbabwe. Visit www.nationaltrust.org.nz or www.historic.org.nz for details. It's best to join in New Zealand because the cost to join once you get to the UK is comparatively astronomical. Many National Trust attractions will appeal to children, such as the Beatrix Potter Gallery in Hawkshead and Lacock Abbey in Wiltshire, location for Hogwarts in the Harry Potter movies.

From Isaac's journal: 'Yesterday we went to the Louvre and saw the Mona Lisa, but apart from that it was very dull.'

It is important to remember that there are a huge number of exciting and interesting things that you can do either free or cheaply. Allow plenty of time to research these budget-friendly outings, but word of mouth recommendations en route are also a good way to get tips from other travellers.

Some of our favourite 'freebies' included Dune de Pyla (France), an enormous sand dune on the west coast of France that is much more fun than it sounds; Greenwich (London) with its park and associated museums, especially the Royal Observatory and National Maritime Museum; the Bom Jesus do Monte steps (Braga, Portugal); the street theatre on Las Ramblas (Barcelona, Spain); the kids' interactive science gallery at the National Museum of Scotland (Edinburgh); and Hamleys Toy Store (London) although you will almost certainly be asked to buy something there. There are also cheaper alternatives to expensive activities, e.g. walk up the stairs of the Eiffel Tower rather than take the lift. Our kids loved the Eiffel Tower and by walking up, and going with one or other parent, we were able to take them up three times.

Another important consideration when planning your sightseeing is to choose fewer and better quality examples of activities in order to avoid doing too much of the same kind of thing.

Visions of the United Kingdom. Karen still has plenty of relatives there, several of whom we visited, and my great-grandparents all came out from the UK to New Zealand. It was very interesting for the children to get an idea of their ancestral lines.

(Above) What happens when you arrive somewhere late and everyone is too tired to be bothered going out for dinner? Floor picnic in a cheap hotel room in Lorca, Spain. Cucumber, watermelon, olives, cheese, chorizo and, of course, red wine.

(Right) Dordogne, France. The reality is that most of the trip was really, really nice.

Chapter 6:
Reality check

This chapter is vitally important to your understanding of what prolonged family travel will be like. Travelling with your kids is a little bit like giving birth – while you can recall that it hurt, given some time what tends to stick with you is the wonder of the gains that resulted from that pain. And although there is no physical pain involved in travelling with your family, it *can* be emotionally draining. Be prepared for times when you might start to question yourself about why you are towing these small citizens around and why you haven't just left them on a bus somewhere. What you need to remember is that the benefits further down the track are enormous and definitely worth the effort.

We instigated a 'no blame' policy that we put in place well before we left home. It came about because we knew in advance that things would go wrong from time to time, e.g. one of us choosing a lousy restaurant, getting lost, leaving something behind, or whatever – so we decided there would be no point in apportioning blame when nothing constructive could come of it. It almost made it humorous when one of us got things wrong, e.g. 'Thank goodness this is a No Blame Tour because otherwise you guys might be really hacked off with me,' the person concerned would chuckle.

Challenges and opportunities

Probably the hardest part of a family OE is being together 24 hours a day, seven days a week and often in close physical proximity. When either of the adults needs a break from the children or, for that matter, from the other adult, they may be hard-pressed to find an opportunity. Adapting to the habits and pace of children can be difficult, too.

Petty though it sounds, I found one of the hardest things to get used to was having the children repeatedly step in front of me or cross my path while we were out walking. It drove me nuts on more than one occasion. However, I kept it to myself because I knew it was my problem and that kids have a different sense of space than adults. In any case, the children began to do it less as they acquired the knack of picking a line on the busy streets of some of the world's biggest cities.

Ironically, having your family with you 24/7 is also your special chance to spend time with the family, on holiday, away from the pressures of work, and enjoying the thrill of overseas exploration. More than anything, it's an opportunity to really get to know your children. For many parents, the biggest insight they get into their children's typical day at school is the words 'Not much' in response to their asking what has been going on in their lives. But now you are about to share all their experiences and you'll be able to exchange observations and even jokes about it as a family. When you return home, you will have a store of shared experience that is likely to form a life-long bond.

A friend of mine told me, 'Working is just about buying time to do what you want'. So treasure the time you have bought yourself. There is plenty of time to talk, time to look, time to think, time to write, time to do things that you never had time for at home.

No two families are the same, however, so consider how well suited your family will be to spending a great deal of time together. Maybe you will need more space, in which case apartment-style accommodation may suit you; spend more time in each location if the travelling is likely to make your family fractious. If the budget allows, consider taking a nanny! But seriously, if you foresee problems, take time to work around them, and be prepared to adapt your plans along the way.

By the time we reached Italy, towards the end of our trip, we were tired of being constantly on the move. So instead we picked fewer locations, spending more time in each and staying in better-quality accommodation.

From Karen's journal: 'Treat of all treats, some time to myself to take photographs and visit the Catedral del Apóstol. Then totally self-indulged with a solo glass of vino tinto and a Gitanes in a small bar, listening to guitar players in the street.'
Santiago de Compostela, Spain

As parents of young children you're probably already familiar with the phrase 'I'm bored'. Try not to let this influence you unduly, particularly if you find yourselves feeling just a tiny bit guilty for uprooting your children and dragging them away from their friends and everything they are used to. You'll have to do a certain amount of figuring out as you go whether it is worth persevering with a particular strategy in the face of disgruntled children or whether it might be best to give in to their pressure and move on to something new. You can always console yourself with the fact that generally speaking they are not feeling bored out of spite, and if you can't convince them to relax and let you enjoy your moment, then they are probably sufficiently tired or unhappy to warrant getting your attention.

From Isaac's journal: 'Went to
Acropolis today. Big stone thing with
pillars and friezes. We went into the
museum full of Acropolis artefacts.
Nothing interesting there. On the way
back we went to Temple of Olympian
Zeus. It was just a pile of pillars but
there were some cute puppies.'

Prepare for compromise and self-sacrifice

It is a fact of life that when you travel as a family you have to be prepared
to compromise on a number of things; most often these will include
where you go and what you do. This can feel a bit frustrating at times
when you have to head home early to get tired children into bed, while

*Enjoying a gyros
pita at an outdoor
cafe in Heraklion,
Crete. It was
around 10.30 pm
but the children
quickly adapted to
taking an evening
promenade, having
a drink in a bar and
eating later.*

what you really want to do is explore some of those exotic-looking cafes and bars you've passed during the day.

One of the main discoveries of our trip was the degree to which children will directly or indirectly dictate the terms of the OE. We all know that if our children are happy, then we will be happy, and the converse applies, but what is less well known is that this truism is thrown into stark relief when you are travelling as a family in close proximity, sometimes for months on end. Don't fight it, just work within it to get a happy result for all involved.

You can still take advantage of some of those fabulous establishments that beckon to you. It should be possible to get your children used to going to bed later; this is normal practice for most families in southern Europe. Once the children are used to being up later, there's no reason why you can't take them with you when you want to go out in the evening, especially if you resort to bribery: a stroll in the warm night air can incorporate an ice cream somewhere along the way.

Fries, too, can be your friend. If you have your heart set on a leisurely drink in a cafe while you watch exotic Europeans float by, order a plate of fries/*patatas fritas*/*pommes frites* and your children will be happy for a short time. Most countries in Europe appear to offer a version of the humble fried potato chip, thank goodness, and I've never yet met a kid who didn't like them!

From Luke's journal: 'I took a 30 minute walk to the lighthouse which was really nice. Got to walk at my own speed, go where I wanted and didn't get pushed or grabbed or hassled for a while.'
San Pedro de Moel, Portugal

It's particularly hard when you are planning an outing that the adults will love, but which elicits less enthusiasm from the children. Just as you might do at home, create an incentive. It might be a reward in the picnic or a promise to trade the outing for a later trip that will please them. ('I'll take you back to that swimming pool you loved if you go on this walk with me.') Another ploy is to point out that they never know what they'll find along the way and that it could turn out to be the best adventure ever. Remind them of previous times when reluctance has turned to rapture because of some unexpected discovery. Incentives are powerful; but you alone will know how far you can push this tactic, as reluctant whining children will almost certainly ruin any outing.

When we stayed at Glen Nevis Youth Hostel, at the base of Ben Nevis, the highest mountain in the UK, we were rewarded with a beautiful day. We announced to the children that we were going to hike up a valley nearby to see a waterfall, and were answered with groans and protestations along the lines of 'I don't want to' and 'That's boring'. Ignoring these, we trudged off up the valley and enjoyed one of the most beautiful walks of our trip. However, what got the children revved up (not the scenic beauty, I can assure you) was a three-strand wire bridge across the river and a great swimming hole. They crossed and re-crossed the wire bridge multiple times, and spent a good 20 minutes cavorting and diving in the icy water. It was all great fun and afterwards the children grudgingly agreed that it had been a good outing.

> From Pearl's journal: 'We walked up Mount Snowdon and swam in two of the three lakes. I liked the second one best because the first one was too cold. I ate lots of chocolate and got worn out because we walked too far. I did some cross-country walking and stood in lots of sheep poos.'

Caught short

You've just arrived at the station to catch a train out of town, everyone has their pack on their back, the train leaves in five minutes and there's a queue for tickets. Then a little voice says, 'I need to pee'. As everyone knows, when a child has to go, they have to go. Not in half an hour but NOW! There's a frantic scramble to locate a public toilet, and then they get stage fright and can't produce. Bless them!

You can't always avoid this scenario, but you *can* insist that children visit the toilet before you leave on any outing so they become used to emptying their bladder on demand. Always carry toilet paper with you along with a ziplock plastic bag in case you were too late and need somewhere to put damp undies. You also need to carry loose change because many toilets in Europe charge a small fee in return for keeping the facility clean. It's common sense to avoid going barefoot into any public toilet, which is when jandals or similar come in very useful. Another useful tip is to ration drinks on long journeys if you know there will be no toilet facility available. And always accompany children into a toilet building, or stand outside and have them talk to you so you can be sure they are safe.

With all those late nights and steady travelling, you need to catch up sometime.

Destination travel

'When do we get there?' We all know that question well as it drifts forward from the back seat of the car. This is matched on family travels by 'What are we doing today?'

Kids want to know where they are going, why and what's in it for them. They will very quickly get restless and behave annoyingly if there is no set destination. Try to give them a time and a destination or plan at the start of each day, even if it means you have to make it up as you go along or have to change the plan later.

It was our experience that the prospect of taking a stroll for the fun of it to see where we ended up never got a positive reaction from the kids. We did it anyway, but had to coax them along with promises of a drink, an ice cream or a swim along the way.

> From Isaac's journal: 'Today we drove a heck of a long time until we came to Portugal.'

We would discuss plans as we were driving or in the evening when the children had gone to sleep. That way, we were united in what we told them and showed that we knew what we were doing. That's important to children as they are out of their depth and need the parents to be in control. Once we'd told them exactly where we were going that day, they would quiz us on it, and we would aim to have done our homework sufficiently to be able to convince them of its wonders.

It is difficult for children not to get bored when you have to spend time finding parking, accommodation, food, comfort stops and the like. At times like this, they have to sit or stand around and wait so it pays to have handy books or portable games to keep them entertained.

We made our children walk a lot and they soon became fit enough to scarcely notice 3–4 km trips on foot. If your kids are the right age for it, walking is ideal, but it does require planning for water, food and rest stops.

Morte de
S. Francisco
de Assis

Tiled fresco in the city of Porto, Portugal. It was a very
pleasant surprise to come around a corner and suddenly
be confronted by whole walls of beautiful tile work.

With all the moving around, sightseeing and stimulation involved in family travel, sometimes the best thing you can do is to take a day or two off in between major excursions. How you do this will, of course, largely depend on your accommodation at the time. Don't be afraid to give them a day in front of the TV, or just sitting around playing games or reading.

From Isaac's journal: 'We swam and played, then went for a walk in the town, and then swam and played.'

Montignac, France

See the world from a different point of view

Integral to the No Blame Tour policy is not blaming your children for what you, as adults, can't do. It is important to appreciate that children's needs must come first and any sacrifices you might have to make en route are likely to be compensated for by seeing things through your children's eyes. They will appreciate sights, moments and elements of the trip that you may not even notice (another reason for them to keep a journal because they will note things in there that you will treasure forever).

From Karen's journal: 'We are sitting on the balcony in Cordoba after a long car drive. It's 40 degrees and we've just walked with our packs a long way to our rooms when Pearl says, "You know, sometimes life just amazes you!"'

Having the children with you will allow you to have experiences that you may never have enjoyed as an adult traveller so keep an eye open for these chances.

When we visited Hania, Crete, the owner of the pension where we stayed for three nights offered to take us out for a day 'in order to educate the children'. George, a truly wonderful man, drove us to a beach 'where real Cretan people go'. On the way, he pointed out interesting places and offered snippets of history, and gave us a hint of what it was like to live in modern-day Crete.

Later he took us up into the valley above the beach to his home, a restored 400-year-old property where local olives used to be pressed for oil. He proudly showed the children the original stones that were used for pressing the olives – it was a great little lesson for the kids in local history and we could really feel the age of the equipment. George gave us lunch: fried fresh sardines, chicken and tomato casserole, salad and fresh bread, which we enjoyed in the shady stone porch of the house along with some local wine before retiring for a siesta. The children, however, soon became restless and so George took us up to his local village where we drank coffee and chatted to some of his friends.

We all then climbed back into George's car and went up further into the hills to see some original wells established by the Turks in the thirteenth century. All the while George regaled the children with interesting snippets of history – he worked very hard in his role of teacher-for-a-day.

Finally, he drove us back past all the new houses being built by the British, letting us know in no uncertain terms how he felt about this invasion, eventually delivering our exhausted but well-informed family back to the pension.

During your travels, your children will appreciate the many opportunities to keep 'grown-up' hours, as well as adult-style activities such as eating at restaurants, visiting bars, and talking to other adults. By thinking and acting inclusively with your children you will enjoy your trip all the more, as well as get to know your children in new ways.

Finding time for yourself can be tricky. Karen and I would give each other a half-day off occasionally and we also split up the children when we felt they needed a break from each other. This was a good chance to do things that other members of the family might not have been interested in, e.g. an exhibition or some personal shopping time. Interestingly, the children chose to stick together more than we expected, partly for security and partly for fear of missing out on some adventure that their sibling got to enjoy. Karen and I also got some time together without the children when relatives or friends were able to babysit, but those times were few and far between.

Opportunities for adult intimacy will be severely limited by the close confines in which you will probably find yourselves. A bit of furtive snogging in unusual locations can be fun in itself but prepare yourself for some enforced abstinence.

Food

For most people, children included, eating is truly one of the great pleasures in life, and there is so much scope for enjoyment when travelling. However, finding what you want, when you want it, and at a reasonable price can present opportunities for family strife.

Frayed tempers can develop when confronted with a variety of choices, especially after hours of walking. Kids don't care what the cost is when they are hungry and they don't appreciate their parents dragging them away from what seems to them a perfectly reasonable establishment just because the adults don't like the price, the food on offer or, worst of all, the 'ambience'. Whether they get dessert or not will probably be the children's main concern.

Whenever possible, we tried to spot a restaurant while we were out during the day or made a choice from a guide book. This would spare us the walking around and looking at dinner time, to the immense relief of the children.

You just have to take your chances with most restaurant choices, and it is usually the parents who will feel disappointed or ripped off if the choice is not good. Most of the time, the children don't notice and tend to be choosing simpler dishes that don't often disappoint. Because choosing an eatery was a prime area for family strife, we made sure we rigorously applied the No Blame Tour strategy.

It is important to remember that eating out can be the source of some wonderful memories from your trip, and not always because of the quality of the food. The service you receive, the people you meet and the surroundings/view can all make it a memorable experience. If you're really lucky, the food will be great too. (We have included some of our favourite eating-out stories in Chapter 9.)

'Anything that has sugar in it is bound to be good. For example, Irn-Bru has enough sugar in it to strip the plaque off your teeth! Unfortunately, you can only get this drink in Scotland.' Isaac

'Try different foods even if you're not sure that you will like it.' Pearl

Don't forget, opening and closing times vary from country to country. For example, most shops and restaurants/cafes in Spain close at about 3–4 pm and don't open again until much later, usually around 8 pm. And much of Mediterranean Europe enjoys the siesta habit so it can pay to organise any picnic-style lunches before the shops close. In larger centres, however, the supermarkets generally stay open right through.

From Pearl's journal: 'Today we drove to Evora. When we booked into our hostel we found out that the owner had two budgies and a dog. We went to a church made of bones and skulls and it was really gross. For dinner we had meat and snails.'

A common sight as we travelled around Europe – litter strewn around beautiful locations. This time on the road up to the magnificent monasteries of Meteora, Greece.

The reality of returning home

After seven months away, we all became very tired and it seemed that the children's behaviour was testing us more, or perhaps we had less tolerance for it. Either way, the energy we spent on trip administration began to outweigh our enjoyment and we knew it was time to pack it in. It was a hard decision because we knew that once we were home, there was no going back for a long time.

You have to trust your instincts on this one, consider the reasons and discuss it with the whole family before making the commitment to return. Once you've touched down, it quickly becomes apparent that life has continued on without you and you may experience a feeling of culture shock even though you are at home. Your kids may also be experiencing mixed feelings about the return home.

'That's what I love most about New Zealand. It's so full of nothing!'
Isaac

Both children immediately noticed the clean-and-greeness that is so typically New Zealand – they couldn't believe how little rubbish was on the side of the road. They also clung to their bedrooms for a good period of time after our return, happy to just have time at home to read, play with their toys and not have to pack a bag.

Chances are that the children will look forward to getting back to school so that they can catch up with friends after a long drought. You need to explain to them that while they've been away, their friends will have learnt things at school that they haven't but, with your help and the help of their teachers, there will be an opportunity to catch up. It's probably advisable to meet briefly with the teachers before the children start back, so that both teacher and child feel comfortable when these hurdles are encountered.

We tried our best to eat what the locals ate and drink what the locals drank.

(Left) Lunchtime at Üçhisar, Turkey.

(Below) A woman in traditional dress tends her stall at Nazaré, Portugal. The women of Nazaré all wear short skirts because they are expected to help with the launching and retrieval of the fishing boats.

100 soorten bier
bières différentes
kinds of beer

Comparing separatist movements while visiting Ondarroa, deep in the heart of Basque country, Spain. No bombs went off while we were there, but we weren't so far away from explosions when we visited Turkey.

(Right) Early on in the trip, the children just wanted to stick closer to us

Chapter 7:
Personal safety

Most children will be overwhelmed to a greater or lesser extent by the various new environments they find themselves in and the usual reaction will be to stick closely to you. So much 'personal closeness' can be a bit testing for parents.

Karen: Having a child or two literally hanging off me most of the day was certainly a test. It was something I should have predicted would happen but hadn't thought about just how intense it would be. I had to keep reminding myself that we were the only constant in our children's lives. Everything else changed, day to day, minute by minute, which made us their 'rocks' and, like little limpets, they clung to us. I just took a deep breath and focused on enjoying that little hand in mine. In hindsight, this was a very special bonding time and I miss it now that we're home.

Our children took a while to adjust to the cramped confines in underground trains, buses and even crowded streets – we had to remind them to 'stay in your lane'. They kept elbowing people, and commuters in crowded cities don't always see the amusing side of that. The kids were much more aware of their personal space by the end of our trip, having been crushed in enough rush-hour public transport.

Take time before leaving New Zealand to explain to children the different kinds of situations they might encounter, how they might deal with them, and how you, as the adults, will also deal with them. Their teachers will probably have educated them to some extent about 'stranger danger', and you can extrapolate as you see fit.

We became more relaxed as the trip wore on and the children got a lot more confident about separating from us. We learned to trust our instincts, and not once did we feel that our children were really unsafe. In fact, we came to believe that having the children with us made us less of a target for weirdos and thieves.

A lot of the cities you visit will be busier than anything the children may have encountered before so pre-warn them. It's a good idea to come up with some strategies in advance for specific situations, e.g. in the event you get separated. Situations that might arise include children becoming separated and then lost in places such as a busy market, train station, airport, or even on a city street. Having an idea of what to do in the event of a mishap will ensure children are forewarned without being freaked out. And if you have more than one child, impress upon them the importance of looking out for each other.

In the event they became separated from us, we told our kids to not move from the last place they saw us. If we then still couldn't find each other, they were to find a policeman or other official and explain the problem. We tried to make sure that the children always knew the name of the hostel or street where we were staying. Friends of ours instructed their children to find the nearest large hotel or hostel, reasoning that they would have a better chance of finding someone who could speak English there, plus they would have somewhere safe to wait.

It might also pay to warn your children about the hobos, beggars and drunks they will see on city streets in many countries. Most will be harmless, but encourage your children to walk with their heads high and look confident – an approach that will make them, at least to the

Crowds, like those shown here at the Trevi Fountain in Rome, are ideal places for pickpockets or for just losing track of your children in the mass of people. Vigilance is required and walkie-talkies can help.

observer, less of a target. By the same token, reassure them that the majority of people in the world are nice, regular folks just going about their business.

Interestingly, our children made comparisons between how they felt in different cities. London got a bad report – 'No one seems to see us' – whereas they felt more comfortable in Paris, Barcelona and Athens because, even though it was crowded, people appeared to be used to children and were more tolerant. Both kids were very receptive to the ambience of a place and often used their gut reactions to let us know if they felt uncomfortable.

You may wish to emphasise to your children how much valuable time can get wasted if you have to keep stopping to find each other when you could instead be enjoying whatever it was you came to see. They will easily relate to the loss of play-time. However, there may well be times when you choose to split up your little group for whatever reason; just be sure everyone knows where and when you will meet up again.

On our first evening in Lisbon, Portugal, we were in the downtown area when I was approached by a young man who wanted to sell me some hash. I thanked him for the offer and explained I was not in the market, besides which I was here with my family who were a short distance behind. He was very apologetic when he saw the children and quickly moved along to look for new customers. It made for another interesting 'home school' lesson when the children asked me what the man had wanted.

'Stay away from weird people, other than your parents. Around the Moulin Rouge was pretty creepy.' Isaac

Choosing accommodation that will keep you all together is a good option when considering family safety issues. However, this might not always be possible in which case you need to have a plan. For example, if the children are in a separate room, should they lock it from the inside at night, in which case no one can get in – including you? And what will happen if they have to leave their room at night to get to a toilet? One solution to this particular scenario is to request two keys to the room. You might also consider splitting your family so that there's an adult in each room. Most European establishments lock the main door to the building at night so it is unlikely that non-residents will be able to enter the building. Another tip is to choose a room higher up (i.e. not on the ground floor) to avoid entry through a window by an unwelcome visitor. You'll naturally be careful but don't let it overwhelm your enjoyment of the trip.

From Karen's journal: 'London is so widespread and crowded that the children are having a little trouble comprehending my concerns for safety, and our requests for considerate behaviour. Isaac has told me I'm way too uptight and I should relax unless I want to ruin his time away.'

You will find that in many other cultures children are treated differently than they are at home. People are inclined to want to touch and stroke visiting children, perhaps even offer them small treats. While your children might enjoy the extra attention, tell them they do not have to respond if they don't want to, i.e. it's OK to say 'no' as long as they are polite about it.

In Turkey, our small blonde daughter attracted lots of attention. People were constantly touching her hair, pinching her cheeks and offering her presents. This was novel at first, but within a week Pearl was hiding behind us to avoid the unwanted attention of strangers, particularly men. Occasionally, people even requested a kiss from her, at which point we had to explain to her that while these people meant her no harm, it was OK for her to politely decline or for us to do so on her behalf.

Safety regulations

In some countries, you may find that safety precautions are not up to much, especially walking paths and climbing places where you might expect to find safety barriers or at least warnings. Set limits for the children and be prepared to be tough about it.

It would also pay to check age and height restrictions at any theme park you intend to visit in order to avoid disappointed children at what was going to be the BIG visit to Disneyland or Legoland, etc. This information can usually be found on the relevant website.

Looking after your belongings

From Day One, get into the habit of never leaving your bags unattended. There are lots of people out there who, while they wish you no direct harm, are happy to make their living out of stealing your belongings. No matter how hard you try, it is difficult to avoid looking and behaving like a tourist, even more so when you have children in tow. Buy padlocks for your luggage so that they can't be easily accessed during plane, train and bus trips. Some airports offer a shrink-wrap service (probably more to prevent people inserting stuff like drugs than theft) but it's an option worth considering if you have any concerns.

On your arrival at an airport, try to get to the luggage carousel before the bags start coming through. And whenever possible, make sure another family member is watching claimed bags that are already loaded on your trolley. Impress upon the children that they must never leave baggage unattended unless it is an emergency. Once you're out of the terminal, don't load all your luggage into a taxi without one of you (preferably an adult) already being in the vehicle in the event it drives off without you.

Wallets are a favourite target for pickpockets. Keep them in a front pocket, ideally a zipped pocket, or use a money belt. Women's bags should be of the type that can be carried over the shoulder or used as a backpack (although you should be aware that people often nab stuff out of backpacks in crowded situations such as the Tube or Metro – a small padlock or even a twist tie on the zips can discourage this). Don't flash around your camera, MP3 player or phone any more than necessary, which can be difficult when you are trying to be a tourist enjoying your day out. In other words, watch your stuff. And, importantly, get some insurance so that, in the worst-case scenario, you can replace what you lose. What can't be replaced are photos and diaries so protect those with a passion.

I'd been to Naples, Italy, once before on which occasion my friend had her wallet stolen on a crowded bus. So it came as no surprise on this family trip to see large signs at the train station warning us to 'Protect your belongings' and 'Pickpockets operating in this station'. When we arrived, I downed all my packs for a rest and got out my wallet to buy some water from a small kiosk on the platform. It surprises me now that I couldn't feel several pairs of eyes on the back of my head. Next moment, the train arrived and my mind jumped to the task of getting everyone safely aboard. In the process I became wedged between two men who were trying to get in. Then, just as the doors were about to close, and we were smiling with relief at having got ourselves aboard safely, two more men quickly exited before the train pulled out. Five minutes later, I was looking out the window at Naples passing by when my hand brushed past my pocket in which there was NO wallet-shaped lump. I checked it – and all my other pockets – but knew almost at once I had been a dumb tourist who had lost his wallet to the pickpockets. It was a tough way to learn, especially because it was another 40 minutes before the train stopped, at which point the operator at the credit card helpline kindly informed me that the thieves had made purchases to the tune of €1500 in the time that it had taken me to get to a phone.

Internet safety

Unless you take a laptop with you, you'll probably have to use Internet cafes frequently to send and receive e-mail. Do consider carefully what you send and receive in terms of private information, especially anything to do with Internet banking as software that can subsequently track your keystrokes can be present on public computers.

Your children should already be familiar with staying safe on the net but it's worth checking they know the rules (there are plenty of websites with guidelines, e.g. www.teamup.co.nz if you're not sure where to start). When the budget allows, you could let children access approved games on the net while you sit alongside them to write e-mails.

No-go areas

Guide books and local information offices are always good indicators to areas in a town that are best avoided. Local knowledge is the best source of information but, as tourists, you can't always access that. The other side of this coin is that seedy areas are sometimes good fun to visit, even with the children.

Driving

If you choose to drive at any time, there are some added risks to consider. The first involves adjusting to driving on the right-hand side of the road – not always an easy task.

We quickly settled into the roles of driver and navigator respectively. Nonetheless, it took a concerted team approach with the children singing from the back seat, 'Right-hand side of the road, Right-hand side of the road' to make sure we survived all the intersections, roundabouts and one-way systems. And while we had a few hiccups, we all got a laugh out of the occasional wrong way around a roundabout or against the flow in a one-way street. Fortunately there were no accidents and I suspect we also provided a bit of entertainment for the locals. Drivers in Europe, we found, were incredibly helpful and considerate. They make an effort to allow room for you and have a live-and-let-live attitude that is very refreshing.

Then there's parking. In the larger centres there are generally plenty of parking buildings available, but they will empty your wallet faster than a Naples pickpocket. On the plus side, they tend to be covered by CCTV surveillance, providing a safe and secure parking option. Always take anything of value with you when you leave the car, and in the event of having to leave luggage behind, lock it in the boot or do your best to make sure it is out of sight.

Our car was sufficiently old to not attract attention from potential thieves and you may want to consider that when renting or purchasing during your travels. A shiny new Peugeot would be worth pinching, but a 1992 Ford Mondeo with one hubcap missing? I think not . . .

From Luke's journal: 'Isaac is quite nervous about all the scary people in our street. Good for him to see that life is not all ice creams and pizza for the rest of the world.'

Lisbon, Portugal

Sometimes, it's as nice as it looks in the brochures and movies.

(Above and right, top) The island of Santorini, Greece. Paradoxically, one of the most litter-strewn places we visited.

(Right, bottom) Sun-worshippers on the Greek island of Corfu. It was a relief to be away from the blistering sun of New Zealand.

Karen and I fell in love with Paris (again!) because, amongst other recommendations, there always seemed to be surprises around the corner. In this case, the hunting horn band, dressed in their bright red coats and gleaming boots, playing a few family favourites on a Saturday afternoon.

(Right) Taking in the Henry Moore sculptures at the Yorkshire Sculpture Park, Wakefield, England. Great fun for the kids to be able to climb into, onto, over and under some famous fine art.

Chapter 8:
So, how was the trip?

The trip was wonderful, exciting, boring, magnificent, hard, adventurous, fun. It was no harder than we had expected, but no easier either. It was as fabulous as we had hoped it would be, even though we were exhausted by the end.

What was it like from a kid's point of view?

Kids adapt quickly to new situations and they take things in their stride, probably better than adults do. They're not always comparing the places or experiences to others they have had or how they wanted things to be. They tend to take it all at face value, which is a nice way to travel.

From Isaac's journal: 'I've been to the Leaning Tower of Pisa! Hmm, I can't quite get over it that I can say that!'

We have found that the children don't really discuss or contemplate the trip to any large degree. They are aware of the magnitude of what they have done but don't really have a context into which they can put it. As time goes by, they relate more and more of their travel experiences to things that happen day-to-day, but there is no magical transformation or result that you can point to and say, 'See, the children are so much better for this experience.' It's just a feeling that we have that we have evolved as a family and the children can't help but be subtly different from what they would have been without this trip. This is also confirmed from talking to other parents who have done a family OE.

The 'culture' of our family changed for the better as a result of the trip. Our children, who were old enough to remember specific details about it (often more than we can), refer back to their experiences regularly. They get excited when they recognise a place they have been on TV and they use some of their French or Spanish words as a matter of course. Overall, they seem more grounded and more confident.

Every day they were experiencing the sort of things that would be a once-a-week or once-a-month moment at home. I likened the experience to being plugged into the experience 'mains' for eight months.

We wouldn't hesitate to recommend a trip like this to other families. Travel is a superb way for the family to bond, and to create a wealth of shared experiences to draw on. But we would strongly suggest you heed some of our advice – hence the book.

'If you can't stand boredom, don't attempt this trip. I also definitely got homesick. I really missed my friends.'
Isaac

But now it's time to stop giving advice and to offer some of our favourite stories to give you a taste of what the trip was like. We're not suggesting you necessarily visit these places, but it may help you to decide just where to stick that first pin in your map.

The children's favourite moments

Here is a selection of highlights from the children's perspective on some of the activities, events or attractions that made an impression on them and gave them the most fun. We found the fun factor increased with the amount of interactivity. And all of these activities had educational value, but shhhh!, don't tell them that! We have also indicated which activities are free for when you need a cheap day.

EuroDisney, Paris, France. www.disneylandparis.com
Pearl: 'We spent 10 hours at EuroDisney. My favourite rides were the Buzz Lightyear and Orbatron and Thunder Mountain. And I loved the Christmas parade and the Haunted House.'

Eiffel Tower, Paris, France. www.tour-eiffel.fr/teiffel/uk/
Isaac: 'We walked up to the first floor which had a lot of displays of the features of the tower. On the third floor (which you had to take the lift up to) there were displays of the rooms in the tower. At night we saw the tower all lit up, it was orange and it flashed, and there were lots of people selling flashing Eiffel Tower souvenirs.'

Catacombs, Paris, France. www.catacombs.explographies.com/
Pearl: 'We went underground into some catacombs and saw lots of skulls and bones. It was fun but a bit spooky.'

Cité des Sciences, Paris, France. www.cite-sciences.fr/english
Isaac: 'There was a *Star Wars* exhibition, optical illusions and loads of animation things like sonic recognition. There was a submarine with a periscope.'
Pearl: 'We also went to a Maths section. In this place was a room that used centrifugal force and Mummy felt sick afterwards. We also went to an imagery place where you could lend the *Mona Lisa* your voice to make her speak.'

Arras Tunnels, Arras, France. www.france-for-visitors.com/north/arras.html

Isaac: 'We went into these tunnels beneath the church that were over a thousand years old. In the First World War, British soldiers dug 14 km to get behind enemy lines.'

Pearl: 'And guess what? New Zealanders helped dig the tunnels!'

Grand Dune de Pyla, France. www.dune-pyla.com FREE

Isaac: 'We had to climb up to the top but I roly-polyed down. The dunes have covered a hotel and part of our campground.'

Vézere River, Dordogne, France. www.canoesvalleevezere.com/

Isaac: 'We hired some kayaks and saw dead eels, fish and a big chateau. I was in a kayak with Mummy, it took us three hours.'

Oceanário de Lisbon, Portugal. www.oceanario.pt

Isaac: 'The oceanarium was divided up into four smaller zones. They were the Arctic, the Pacific, the Atlantic and the Indian. In the central tank there were sharks, grouper, a sunfish and a manta ray. There were also otters, jellyfish, octopus, crabs, starfish, anemones and lots of stinky students.'

Bom Jesus do Monte, Braga, Portugal. FREE

Isaac: 'We climbed a lot of stairs (116 metres) to a chapel place; along the stairs there were scenes depicting the stations of the cross.'

Boat ride, Porto, Portugal

Isaac: 'We went on a boat ride up the Douro River and saw six bridges and lots of port companies. The woman told us that farming in the Douro valley is nine months of winter followed by three months of hell.'

Teatre-Musea Dalí, Figueres, Spain. www.salvador-dali.org

Isaac: 'The Salvador Dalí Museum had lots of art, there was a room called the Mae West room. The furniture made up Mae West's face.'

Las Ramblas, Barcelona, Spain. FREE (or nearly)

Isaac: 'Las Ramblas has the best street theatre artists. We saw ballet dancers, butterflies, aliens, trees, fruit salad, and a coal miner. When you put a coin in their hat they do something funny.'

Sagrada Familia, Barcelona, Spain. www.sagradafamilia.org/eng

Isaac: 'We went to the Sagrada Familia, it was big and colourful but not finished. You really have to go there to realise how incomplete it is.'

Casa Batlló, Barcelona, Spain. www.casabatllo.es

Isaac: '. . . we took the Metro to a house designed by Gaudí. I can really only describe it by saying nothing was straight, everything was colourful.'
Pearl: 'It is interesting because he hardly ever put any straight lines in his buildings.'

London Eye, England. www.londoneye.com/

Pearl: 'On the London Eye we had a guide who pointed out famous buildings. His name was Ed.'

Tate Modern, London, England. www.tate.org.uk/modern/

Pearl: 'The electronic guides were pretty cool because they had quizzes. One painting had a giant sunflower that was attacking some maidens and the guide asked which one of these flowers was attacking the girls and you had to choose from four flowers. I chose the sunflower.'

St Paul's Cathedral, London, England. www.stpauls.co.uk

Pearl: 'We went to the Whispering Gallery but you could hardly hear anyone. I did a worksheet and got an Easter egg as a prize. We went up to the Golden Gallery, we climbed 531 steps to the top. Then we went down to the crypt. We saw the grave Nelson was in and some statues. One had no arms and no legs.'

What did the kids love? Just what you might expect: (Above) Legoland Windsor in England; (Below, left) EuroDisney in Paris; (Below right) Parc Astérix in Paris. These were expensive outings but money well spent considering we spent a whole day at each and the kids raved about them.

Legoland, Windsor, England. www.lego.com

Isaac: 'You could build your own cars and race them. We saw a movie in 3D called *Spellbreaker*, then there was a mini-land which had France and Sweden and England and America and Scotland all made out of Lego. We went on a ride called the Dragon and the actual Dragon smelt of chips. I built a set called the Turbo Turtle.'

Roald Dahl Museum and Story Centre, Buckinghamshire, England. www.roalddahlmuseum.org

Pearl: 'They had touch-screen computers and you could make your own postcards and your own bookmarks. I made one of each and they gave you a little booklet. You could make your own character and movie and rhymes and stories and you could dress up. Two men read out stories and acted as well. When they did *The Three Little Pigs*, they were so funny.'

Geevor Tin Mine, Cornwall, England. www.geevor.com/

Pearl: 'The guide took us through the old mine factory and showed us the shaking tables where they put gravel and water on the table which had ridges. The metal was heavy and got stuck on the ridges. Ernie took us through an old mine but when we got a quarter of the way through Karen freaked out so Ernie took her out.'

Eden Project, Cornwall, England. www.edenproject.com/

Pearl: 'When I came out of the humid temperature biome, which is a big dome with a honeycomb pattern on it, my t-shirt was damp because I had been sweating. The biomes have plants in them, tropical plants in the humid biome, and I was doing a worksheet in the humid biome but it got too wet and mushy.'

St Fagans Natural History Museum, Cardiff, Wales. FREE www.museumwales.ac.uk

Pearl: 'St Fagans is 110 acres big. It had old houses you could go into and they smelt bad. I liked the gift shop.'

Welsh Slate Museum, Llanberis, Wales. FREE
www.museumwales.ac.uk/en/slate/
Isaac: 'I got to turn off the water wheel when the museum closed. We saw a blacksmith making dragons.'

Inverness Highland Tattoo, Scotland. www.tattooinverness.org.uk/
Isaac: 'There was dancing and music as well as a motorbike stunt team that drove through two flaming haystacks. Then they brought in a cannon and fired off two rounds. Then I went and looked at the gun display. There was a bazooka and two rifles and two machine guns.'

Topkapi Palace, Istanbul, Turkey. www.kultur.gov.tr/en
Pearl: 'Today we went to Topkapi where the architecture is amazing and the jewels are stunning and they were all just amazing.'

Rahmi M Koc Industrial Museum, Istanbul, Turkey.
www.rmk-museum.org.tr/
Isaac: 'It had lots of old cars, a pink Cadillac, boats, trams, planes, a submarine and lots of models, the bridge of a ship, free Internet and computer games like flight simulator and a car game. We spent five hours there.'

Grand Bazaar, Istanbul, Turkey. www.grandbazaarturkey.com FREE ENTRY
Pearl: 'It's sort of like a maze with loads of beautiful shops. They had belly-dancing shops and shops for all sorts of things. Mummy and Daddy got an evil eye, Isaac got a dagger and I got a little crystal mosque.'

Olympos Chimera, Cirali, Turkey. FREE
Isaac: 'We walked around a curve and suddenly could see all this fire coming out of the rocks. This happens because very flammable gas seeps out of the rock and bursts into flame on contact with the air. This fire is the original Olympic flame. I should have burnt my school socks in the flames.'

Limnoupolis, Hania, Crete, Greece. www.limnoupolis.gr/

Pearl: 'We went to Limnoupolis which was a really cool water park. First we went on all the hydroslides, and then we floated around a big river. Then we had lots of fun on the little kids' stuff and the flying fox which you drop into the water from.'

Leaning Tower, Pisa, Italy. http://torre.duomo.pisa.it

Pearl: 'Got up early and climbed Tower of Pisa. When you're climbing you can't so much feel the lean but it's really scary when you get to the top.'

Pompeii Archeological Site, Naples, Italy. www2.pompeiisites.org

Pearl: 'Today we went to Pompeii which was really spectacular because most of the houses were in ruins but you could still see the walls. We went past what we thought was the bakery and the brothels. I found out that Romans thought up pedestrian crossings.'

Isaac: 'There were a lot of bricks and straight roads and crossings. There was a theatre and gladiator barracks, and baths with body casts.'

Great Wolf Lodge, Niagara Falls, Canada. www.greatwolflodge.com

Isaac: 'I want to go back there. They have fantastic sugary breakfasts. When you walk into the pool area, water goes slop slop on your head.'

This little piggy went to market

Some of our top family time was spent in the markets of Europe.

Carcassonne, France

This market was also full of cheap clothes, toys and assorted hardware, and frequented by numerous North Africans, giving it a character of its own. The town square boasted its own food and flower market, thronging with friendly merchants. We bought the most delicious rotisserie chicken and potatoes and consumed it beneath the walls of the old castle.

Sesimbra, Portugal

We endeared ourselves to a woman at the local market who sold home-made cheeses. We bought one for lunch, and found it so delicious that we returned the next day to buy two for the road. She remembered Karen from the day before and, despite our not being able to understand the Portuguese, it was obvious that she was proudly telling her friends that we had returned for more of her magnificent cheese. We also got rather curious looks at this same market for buying six sardines – the minimum order usually being a couple of dozen!

Porto, Portugal

This two-storey market was another gem – all the gore of good outdoor butchers, bucket upon bucket of variations on olives, cheeses, spring fruit and vegetables, as well as freshly baked breads.

Istanbul, Turkey

The Grand Bazaar is like the world's biggest tourist shop but so much more. It's not quite as charming as it was 20 years ago but remains one of the ultimate market experiences.

When things go right

Areia de Branca, Portugal

After a few days of inland cities, we dreamt of staying in a hostel near a beautiful, sandy swimming beach. We drove down the Portuguese coast from Braga towards Lisbon, searching for the ideal location, but as the day wore on we became more and more overwhelmed by the grubbiness of the beaches. One spot, described in our travel guide as a lovely, salty-dog seaside town, turned out to be a rubbish-strewn wasteland of high-rises and construction sites, the beach littered with rusty tin cans. We drove on, trying other towns along the way. Then finally, at about 3 pm, eureka! We checked out a Youth Hostel at Areia de Branca, a little bay well off the tourist trail, and to our delight it was right in front of a clean, sandy beach. We swam, snoozed and enjoyed a cold beer at a local bar waiting for the hostel to open. Booking in involved mounds of Portuguese paperwork but, for a small surcharge, we were able to secure the family room which was a four-roomed apartment with luxurious bathroom, towels, bedding, mini kitchen, comfy double bed and Sky TV. The window overlooked both the beach and the local bar, so we could slope off for a beer knowing that if the kids needed us (if they ever looked up from the TV screen), they could wave out the window to get our attention. In the morning, the children socialised over their Coco Pops with some Canadian travellers while Luke had a swim. It was definitely the best hostel we had stayed in, equal to a three-star hotel, and we only wished we could have stayed longer.

Üçhisar, Turkey

Having both visited Turkey before, we felt this country could provide our children with their biggest travelling challenge since, in all respects, it is so different from home. We used the Internet to book accommodation in advance from London so we could make things as easy as possible for the children (and, therefore, us).

Üçhisar, in the Cappadocia region of Kayseri, is famous for its exceptional landscape of 'fairy chimneys', cave-houses and underground cities. We arrived late in the afternoon, dead-beat and hungry after having travelled about 18 hours from Istanbul.

The house was an unbelievably good find – a bit costly for Turkey but worth every euro, with two bedrooms, a full kitchen, huge bathroom, lounge and deck, plus bedding and towels. It was built on the remains of a cave-house that dated back to the early Christian settlement, circa 1200 AD. The dark caves spooked the children, but the house itself was sunny and clean, if a bit of a rabbit warren with low stone doorways that threatened Luke's head. We slept surrounded by history in a town that was as interesting as it was beautiful.

The crowning glory was the balcony, with its almost indescribable view over Üçhisar castle, the highest point in the Cappadocia region,

The view from our balcony in Üçhisar, Turkey. It's a dreamy landscape that we never tired of looking at. The kids loved the opportunity to relax in one place for a week, and got a big kick out of the pigeons who did aerial somersaults straight in front of us.

and the softly curving hills and valleys, all of which made for a stunning sight at dusk. We ate at local restaurants, shopped at the market and butcher, and Luke visited the barber for a cut-throat shave.

By the end of the week, we had blended in to some degree. The locals knew us by name, we were invited in to see the newest baby born to the town, and even the pedlars had begun to leave us alone. We drank dark, bitter coffee and the kids became experts at tavlar (backgammon). We explored the cave-houses and talked to the camels by the tourist stands. Every morning we'd wave to the hot-air balloons that rose high above the house.

Üçhisar is slowly being bought up by the French, who are renovating the old, dilapidated cave-houses into holiday homes. The upside of this is that there will be rental accommodation available; the downside, of course, is that the Western world is catching up with Üçhisar.

When things go wrong . . . and right

The ups and downs of travel are well illustrated by our two nights in the Spain town of Seville.

We arrived in searing midday heat and set out to find accommodation as we had not booked ahead. Big mistake. Everyone was overheating and Karen and I had one of our few snippy moments of the trip. However, we eventually got a lucky break at the Youth Hostel which had been full.

Once we had settled in and recovered, we bussed back into town and began exploring. Sunset and cold beer brought some relief from the heat, but we were having trouble finding a suitable restaurant. While we were having a drink at a great little bar we found, we couldn't help noticing two young men stroll up to the bar in curious outfits - rolled white head wraps, shorts over tights and layers of shirts. They rapidly despatched a beer each and melted away down a narrow alley. Shortly afterwards, we heard the thud of drums and blasts from brass instruments. As the cacophany increased, curiosity got the better of us, and we found that, only a couple of streets away, a band was gathering cohesion and momentum - and an audience. They were the escort for a holy relic that was hoisted aloft by a dozen or so men who could only be counted by the sight of their feet under a long black shroud. The curiously dressed men were part of a group of 'supporters' whose role appeared to be to clear the way for the procession and to dart into bars along the way in order to swiftly down free drinks before returning to the street to clear the way again. Great job, I thought, and all in God's name!

The procession inched along, led by censer-waving boys, to a mournful tune somewhere between Tijuana brass and a funeral dirge. The music echoed through the narrow streets and our stomachs leapt in time to the drum beats. At each corner, the relic bearers would stop and slowly shuffle their feet under the direction of a procession leader until the mighty load was eased around the tight bend. Then everyone would take a short break for more drinks, a changeover of relic bearers, or just to chat to friends before getting underway again, like a mighty elephant heading towards a distant water hole, serenaded by the beautiful brass. It was a magical, musical, steamy, candlelit night.

We finally gave up on the procession when we found ourselves next to a busy little restaurant. It was around 10.30 pm and we were all starving. The menu had what we needed and we were treated to Manolo, a friendly waiter who doted on the children and encouraged Karen with her Spanish.

After a delicious dinner, the culmination of an adventurous and intriguing evening, we made it back to the hostel and crashed into bed at 1 am. What a day!

The next day, we planned to take the children to a pet market recommended by a travel guide, then visit the famous Alcazar, and finish with a trip to the Plaza de Espana. All these plans were thwarted by a visit to town by the King and a big military parade. We saw a pretty impressive array of tanks, trucks, fighter jets and soldiers, and the kids, particularly Isaac, were thrilled. However, frustration at all the closures and heat exhaustion were beginning to set in, as was hunger and thirst.

We broke cover of the trees to look for a bus back to the youth hostel and what should greet our weary eyes but a large, playing fountain just across the road from a display board announcing that the temperature was 42 degrees C! We headed for the fountain and dipped heads, hands and feet, and then the children just climbed in, clothes and all.

We stood, dripping, at the bus stop for at least 20 minutes before we managed to catch a bus back to the hostel. We spotted a restaurant not too far away from the hostel entrance and made one of those important travel decisions – we've had a tough morning, we're overheated, tired, thirsty and hungry, and we are going to go and buy some food from this establishment no matter what it looks like or how much it costs. Our luck changed and we had a cheap, scrumptious lunch that was washed down with a couple of cold beers and lots of water. *Gambas* (prawns) was the special of the day so we made the most of it and had two plates full.

After a good rest during the afternoon, we ventured back into town and went to a genuine bullfight. The ring throbbed with heat, colour, costumes and music from the resident brass band but it also had an air of fading relevance to it. It is too hard to justify the brutality in this day and age, but I don't regret attending. However, I wouldn't go back. Karen and the kids found it too harrowing and left quite quickly.

We spent the rest of the evening strolling the streets and had a disappointing dinner, just to prove that Seville was still the boss and we, the mere tourists.

Our last laugh was had the next morning as we prepared for departure from that fair, frustrating city. We drove straight into town, laughing as we went about what horrors Seville could possibly have left to throw at us, and succeeded in securing a parking space almost straight away. We had a very pleasant morning strolling the shops and capped it off with a genuine, local cafe where we had coffee for the adults, thick hot chocolates for the children and we all gorged ourselves on *churros* (Spanish doughnut). The final words were left to Pearl - 'That's music to my mouth!'

Seville won that encounter and the Williamsons came second, maybe even third. However, for all the difficulties, we came away with some lasting memories that were really, really good. It can be a tough road but you never know what is around the corner.

Restaurants to remember

While finding somewhere to eat out can be a prime source of stress, restaurant and cafe experiences often turn out to be some of the most memorable. Read on for a sample.

Pisa, Italy

We chose Trattoria La Buca for our evening meal because it was a recommendation in *Lonely Planet* and it was only a street away from where we were staying. What was more, it backed onto the Piazza dei Miracoli, home of the leaning tower.

We were shown through a picture-perfect Italian restaurant, complete with checked tablecloths and booths, and from our table in the courtyard we could see the top half of the tower lit up. The initial signs were good and only improved for Karen when a drop-dead gorgeous waiter brought our menus.

When we had ordered from Mr Handsome, his even friendlier co-worker began to interact with the children, pulling faces and laughing with them. During our delicious meal, he disappeared briefly, only to return with a Pinocchio key-ring as a gift for each of the children. (*Pinocchio* was written in Pisa and all the street vendors sell souvenirs.)

The staff then led the children to the dessert cabinet and charmed them into accepting a dish of *gelati* – very difficult to get our children to accept ice cream!

They were so accommodating of the children and we enjoyed the food so much (and the view of the tower – and the waiter) that we returned the next night.

We enjoyed lovely food and service again, and the owner was even coaxed into doing a little puppet show for the children. After all the kindly service offered by Mr Handsome and Mr Friendly, we left feeling as though we had enjoyed one of the best restaurants in Italy.

Üçhisar, Turkey

On our first night here we dined at the House of Memories, whose menu offered as good a choice as any for our gluten-free girl.

Seated on the balcony, we had a view of the amazing sculpted stone valley that runs from Üçhisar down to Goreme. However, it wasn't the view that made us fall in love with House of Memories; it was the fabulous hosts – a friendly, goofy waiter and an outgoing owner who rushed around, calling out to no one in particular, 'Yes please! Thank you very much! Mamma mia!' When Pearl was stung by a bee, there was a great flurry of activity and apologies, and, as a distraction, a young man from the restaurant did a crazy dance to a Turkish guitar that the waiter couldn't play.

It was great fun and inspired us to return a few nights later for more of the same. On this occasion we were the only customers, and we took time after dinner to sit in one of the carpeted alcoves that boasts pillows and a low table, and sipped apple tea while our dinner settled. A magical combination of personalities and amazing surrounds.

Ribadesella, Spain

Much as we were enjoying Spain, it was not until we arrived in the little coastal town of Ribadesella that we felt we were in amongst a local population going about their business. We were still tourists, of course, but we were at least 'off the trail'.

We had a drink in the plaza and watched as the local children kicked a football around or veered off to chat to their parents, who were taking early evening drinks in the cafes. When it came time to eat, many of the local residents melted away to their homes, but just around the corner we found a bustling restaurant with an accommodating menu. It was actually a *cidreria*, an establishment serving the local cider.

Drinking cider involves a ritual in which short dollops of the drink

It's hard not to enjoy a restaurant with a view of Italy's Leaning Tower of Pisa. The children loved their opportunity to climb the tower but the view of the dessert cabinet was what captivated them.

are poured from a bottle held at arm's length above your head into a pint glass held at arm's length below your head, i.e. about a 1.5-metre drop. Customers would either pour their own or leave it to the waiters whose job it was to keep circulating and keep the drink flowing. The drinkers were required to down the dollop of cider in one go, which was never more than a couple of gulps. They would then go back to smoking, chatting and nibbling their tapas until the waiter returned to pour their next round. It also appeared to be good etiquette to offer the waiter a drink every now and then so it made for a very jolly bar indeed.

It was our first experience of cider drinking in this form and we were too shy to sit down and order up, especially in our hesitant Spanish and with the children. However, we enjoyed the spectacle and the pretty restaurant provided one of our most memorable meals of the trip.

It was our first real go at ordering Spanish food as it is meant to be enjoyed, and the children got into the spirit of experimenting. While Pearl ordered steak, and Karen and I ordered other gastronomic delights, Isaac ordered grilled baby cuttlefish, despite the fact that he had no idea what they were or what they would taste like. He bravely tried the dish but declined to continue, leaving Karen and me to enjoy their exquisite flavour. It was a night for wonderful atmosphere, superb food and successful family travelling.

Lisbon, Portugal

It was lunchtime after a difficult morning, when everyone was hot, hungry, thirsty and scratchy. After searching in vain for an ideal restaurant, we finally fell into the first eatery that looked halfway decent. It turned out to be a busy local place with football on the TV (of course) and everyone giving us a curious, but friendly eye.

Two very young men were running the cafe for a matriarch who was in the kitchen out back and could be heard but not seen. One of them came over to us and presented the menus, which were written (naturally) in Portuguese. When we asked him to explain what the mystery dishes were, he nodded enthusiastically and pointed them out: 'Thees ees feesh, thees ees feesh, thees ees meeeet, and thees ees meeeet, ah . . . thees ees feesh.' He smiled proudly and left us to our decision-making. In the end, we just had to make some guesses.

As it turned out, we had only just ordered when the food for the table behind us arrived and included the most delicious-smelling octopus (we think) dish. We quickly called our waiter back, cancelled one dish we had ordered (through pointing at the menu and shaking our heads and crossing our hands), and pointed at our neighbour's octopus and nodded enthusiastically, adding 'Sim!' (Yes!). This caused much amusement among the local diners but prompted a barrage of matriarchal disgust from the kitchen which, in turn, caused more general amusement. The young men both looked a bit nervous about going back into the kitchen.

We had a delicious meal, it set our day back on track and the children got an extra dessert treat from our young waiter to top it off.

Fetiye, Turkey

We met a family from the Yukon, in Canada, who were travelling through Turkey for five weeks. Their daughter, Ysa, got along very well with Isaac (who was delighted to find an English speaker of his own age).

Karen and I nearly killed ourselves laughing when we overheard Ysa telling Isaac that she hated trailing along behind her parents while they went from restaurant to restaurant, looking at the menus and trying to decide where to eat. 'I know exactly what you mean,' Isaac replied. So beware, you family travellers.

Luke's favourite moments

Mertola, Portugal

I loved our visit to Mertola. It really felt like somewhere unusual and I loved the heat, dust, colours and smells. We visited the abandoned Sao Domingo mine, an eerie hole in the ground where mineral-spattered walls crumbled down into an orange-green toxic lake. We wandered amongst the broken buildings and machinery, gathering trinkets from the dust and comparing the colourful rocks.

We also visited a man-made lake where the children and I jumped off a jetty into the spooky depths, cooling off quickly. As we drove back to Mertola in the midday blaze, we counted the storks' nests, each a prickly crown on the row of lampposts stretching before us.

That night, after a meal that confirmed for us the repetitive nature of Portuguese menus, we retired to a rooftop bar for coffee and drinks. Everything was whitewash, dark night, stars and music. Someone, somewhere, was playing jazz – a rare and welcome treat – and a short, sharp coffee and three bottles of cheap beer had heightened my appreciation of all that surrounded me.

Karen, bless her heart, took the children off to bed and left me to another beer, more music, and the composition of a slightly bewildering letter home.

Montignac, France

Among the many family activities we indulged in, one of my favourites was kayaking down the Vézere river. It was an ad-hoc choice, which we made upon discovering that kayaking was available, and we were greeted with a beautiful sunny day and a gently flowing, sparkling river. We loaded our picnic lunch into the two-seater kayaks and set off at 10 am. With the current behind us, it was an easy paddle, lightly spiced by some shallow rapids before we rounded a bend and came to our first chateau. We negotiated our way around some old stonework in midstream and paddled right under the overhanging walls of the grand castle that towered above us. Water dripped, moss grew and old, damp smells assaulted our noses but then we paddled back out into the sunshine, smiling at the tourists above us.

After some more mini-rapids and watching the local hawks swoop on fish, we came upon our second chateau, which was even more grand than the first. It too was perched right up against the river and sported tourists like gargoyles who happily took our photo as we waved and paddled.

The day was heating up, so we pulled up on the bank near a bridge and

A biology lesson in action: storks' nests adorned many of the lampposts in Mertola, Portugal. We kept our eyes open for any babies awaiting delivery but, alas, none were sighted.

found a shady tree under which we enjoyed our picnic – *très français*!

After a couple more rapid runs and a brief grounding, we arrived at our final destination, hot, tired and happy. For an impromptu outing it had been a super three hours' worth.

Montignac also gave us a great summer's night out (it didn't get dark until 10 pm) when they ran their annual music night during our stay. Around a dozen bands set up in different corners of the village and played from 7 pm. Locals turned out to stroll between performances, dine out, dance, chat and eat ice cream. It was a wonderful evening with some inspired performances ranging from choir to punk rock.

From Luke's journal: 'Had a lovely coffee and icecream, overlooking the beautiful view and felt like I was the guy from the postcard.'
Dordogne, France.

Paris, France

I can't help it, I just love this city. It's the way you walk around the same corner you walked around the day before and find something completely different, fun and snazzy. Markets full of divine food, cheap wine and the chance to use my rusty French. Sinking my teeth into a proper, buttery, flaky croissant. Sitting on our tiny balcony with a Sunday morning coffee and watching the world go by below while Miles Davis's *Kind of Blue* plays in the background. I'm going back.

Catedral del Apóstol, Santiago de Compostela, Spain

The church is a riot of colour, gold, candles, pomp and tourists – practically a comic-book on Catholicism with its overwrought statues of Christ, Mary, angels and assorted biblical stars. It was technicolour worship.

Mount Snowdon, Wales

Swimming in the lake at the top of the Miner's Path, Mount Snowdon. After preparing ourselves for the possibility of sleet and snow when we visited Wales in summer, it turned out that we hit the record hottest day for July – around 36°C with clear blue skies. Friends from Liverpool escorted us on our walk which was breathtakingly beautiful, blazing hot and long at around 10 km for the round journey. What made the day for me and the kids was plunging into the ice-cold lake at the top of the path, all hot and sweaty from the climb. We enjoyed our wallow under azure skies framed by the high peaks of Snowdon. Lovely!

Saint Helens, England

I never knew my maternal grandfather because he died before I was born, but he grew up in Saint Helens. He used to tell my mother that she had no idea how beautiful it was where they lived in Devonport, Auckland, and that it was paradise to him. Having visited Saint Helens, I now understand why he would say that. It's not the most attractive place in the world but I treasured the opportunity to briefly stroll 'his' town and get a feel for what he felt he had escaped.

Istanbul, Turkey

The heat, culture, noise, bustle, people and food. I remember looking back across the Bosphorus, barbecued fish sandwich in hand, admiring the minarets against the skyline as the sun set, while all around us were hustling crowds of Turks preparing for a political meeting, merchants running from police while holding each end of a table complete with a still smoking fish barbecue, and the blare over the loudspeakers of the Islamic call to prayer. And there, amidst it all, were my blond-haired children, remarkably taking it all in their stride. Truly an astounding city.

Loutro, Crete

Having a 'holiday within a holiday' at a picture-perfect Greek harbour with see-through ocean, a taverna-lined bay, and nothing to do but take it easy. We swam, slept, read, slept, swam and ate. We also made some great new friends so it was a winner in many ways and definitely somewhere to revisit.

Barcelona, Spain

Though I enjoy looking at art, not many works touch me at the core. Gaudí's Casa Batlló and Sagrada Familia both made me feel quite emotional. They were outstandingly beautiful, each grand in its own way, and plain intriguing. What a man Gaudí was to have come up with these designs. Gorgeous!

Karen's favourite moments

It's impossible to pick one favourite place, or one experience, because wonder surrounds you in almost everything you do. Here, however, is my 'best of' list.

Best markets: Marché Richard Lenoir in the Bastille district of Paris, in full swing in April, stirs such culinary excitement that you swear you will never eat fast food again. Then there's the bustling Sunday-morning flea market in the Plaka of Athens. But both are outdone marginally by my all-time favourite, the Grand Bazaar in Istanbul, where shopping is a social event, an assault on the senses and next time I'm taking a suitcase!

Best restaurant experience: Any of the *bodegas* and *tapas* bars in Spain. Brilliant food, and an opportunity to speak Spanish.

Best sugary treat: Sfogliatelle at a busy cafe in Naples. Crunchy layers of fine sweet pastry with a creamy filling, washed down with a cappuccino, *malto calde.*

Best music: Parisians dancing the salsa, waltz and tango along the banks of the Seine in autumn, with the lights of passing boats matched by the twinkling of a Frenchman's eye. Laughing and drinking *chai* while I listen to Turkish men in Goreme playing the *suz* to my children. The accordion player who stepped aboard the Paris Métro and played 'La Vie en Rose' – very romantic.

Best photographic opportunity: It's a toss-up between the colours and macabre action of the bullfight in Seville where I had to fight personal ethics, and the stunningly beautiful town of Ia on Santorini where I had to fight the crowds.

Most spiritual moment: Sitting atop a mound of dirt in Üçhisar, Cappadocia, staring at the curvaceous hill formations as they changed colour in the setting sun and thinking that this is surely proof of the existence of God.

Best street theatre: Las Ramblas in Barcelona. Hours of fun and entertainment for the price of a few coins.

Best architecture: Awe-inspiring masterpieces by Gaudí in Barcelona – Casa Batlló and Sagrada Familia. Unbelievable in their conception, and I'm definitely returning to see more.

Best supermarket: Fortinos in Burlington Ontario. Consumerism at its best, a fabulous gluten-free range, and a compliment about my legs from an 84-year-old gentleman propped up with his Zimmer frame.

Best art experience: I can't *possibly* choose just one, so . . . the Dali Museum in Figueres, Spain, for the sheer amazement of being that close to Dali's incredible work; the Frida Kahlo exhibit in Lisbon for evoking raw emotion; Richard Serra's work at the Guggenheim Bilbao, Spain, for a truly interactive experience; Musée d'Orsay for, well, *everything* on a grand scale; and the Peggy Guggenheim collection (Isaac found this a 'snore-fest') for its opulent setting on the banks of the Venetian canals.

Best freebie: Complimentary *raki* and fruit that comes after a meal in the tavernas of Crete, or the Spanish *tapas* served with every drink in the bars of Granada.

Most relaxing spot: Loutro, an idyllic setting on the Mediterranean. No roads, no shops. Azure warm water, friendly Cretans, cold Mythos lagers and a stack of trashy novels. What more could you want?

Best sunset: From halfway up Mount Snowdon overlooking the Snowdonia National park.

Best sunrise: As seen when waking on the train to Ankara and looking out over the arid Turkish landscape. (And it's a rare event for me to even be up at that time!)

Conclusion – just go!

So, there you go. We've attempted to give you the advice, the flavour, the cautionary tales and the framework to build on. We hope that in sharing our experiences with you, we will have either given you inspiration to go on your own family OE or perhaps provided enough insight for you to identify whether or not such a trip is right for your family (or your family is right for the trip!).

Plan carefully and wherever possible involve your children in the planning. Remember, if the children are happy, the parents are more likely to enjoy themselves. Go safely, be prepared to adapt to the conditions and most of all have a wonderful time because that time will go by quickly.

> From Luke's journal: 'I'm getting a little scared that this holiday will be over and done before I'm ready. All those years of planning and preparing, and already London, Bruges, Paris and Brittany are gone.'
>
> Saintes, France

One of Karen's favourite photographic opportunities – the magnificent view over the town of Ia on the island of Santorini, Greece. The views meant very little to the children and they weren't particularly impressed by Santorini.

People watching: (Left, top) Gavalohora village, Crete; (Left, bottom) Goreme cafe; (Right) Matador; (Below) Steps of the Basilica of the Sacré Cœur, Paris.

St Peter's Basilica, Vatican City, Italy. Grander than grand, bigger than big, and we got to see the real Pope at work.

(Right) A beautiful spring day on the south coast of England. We even had a swim.

Further reading

Websites

This is not a definitive list but rather a suggestion of websites to help you get started with your planning. Most of these we've used but some we've discovered while writing this book. We would strongly encourage you to do your own browsing of the Internet to discover other resources relevant to your trip.

Accommodation

www.tripadvisor.com

Traveller reviews and opinions of hotels, holidays and more. Search a specific hostel before booking to read the opinions of fellow travellers. Write your own reviews to advise others. This site gives recommendations for families with young children or teenagers.

www.hostelbookers.com

Search youth hostels and cheap accommodation in over 2000 destinations worldwide.

www.hostelworld.com

Book hostels worldwide and read reviews on hostels.

www.hostels.net

An online network of independent hostels worldwide. Offers a wide range of quality budget accommodation for backpackers and budget travellers in destinations all over the world.

www.lonelyplanetexchange.com/

Information on worldwide accommodation plus budget flights, car hire and guide books. This site has no affiliation with Lonely Planet Guide publications.

www.letsgo.com

Sightseeing advice and up-to-date information on restaurants, hotels, and inns; with 'a commitment to money-saving travel', i.e. this is for the budget backpacker.

www.holiday-rentals.co.uk

A site to help you find the perfect holiday villa or self-catering apartment worldwide. Details given along with photos, plus information given on suitability for children. We used this site a lot and booked some great accommodation with relative security.

www.ownersdirect.co.uk

Choose from a wide selection of self-catering holiday homes, cottages, farmhouses, chalets and guest houses worldwide. Family-friendly accommodation identified. Over 17,000 holiday homes to rent direct from the owner. We booked our Üçhisar house through this site.

http://joomla.servas.org/

A non-profit cooperative network of hosts and travellers with 13,000 open doors building world peace, goodwill, understanding and mutual tolerance. Servas seeks to provide reciprocal opportunities and personal contacts between individuals of diverse cultures and backgrounds. Travellers are hosted in homes at no charge for a maximum of three nights, and encouraged to immerse themselves in the hosts' day-to-day life for that time.

Country Guides

www.lonelyplanet.com

The official site based on the well-known guide books. Search for country-specific information, accommodation, cheap flights and travel articles, and shop online.

www.alltravelingkidsfamilyvacations.com

An online guide to family holidays, last-minute travel destinations with children, lists of all-inclusive resorts, car activities and lots of country-specific articles. The focus is on travel in the USA, but includes other countries as well.

www.travelforkids.com

A family travel guide for planning holiday trips with children as fun adventures. Get tips on kid-friendly 'must sees', discover hidden treasures and learn insider secrets for holidays in Europe, North America, South America, Asia and Africa. Travel for Kids combines fun things to do with practical tips, plus best bets for family hotels, and staff recommendations for children's books about destinations all over the world.

http://studenttravel.about.com (type 'Events' into site search engine)

Search the Event section for a specific country, add in dates and this website will find you festivals, exhibitions and religious holidays so you can plan to be there, or not.

www.tntmagazine.com

An online magazine dedicated to London. Lists events and has a classified section for jobs, accommodation, and more.

www.bbc.co.uk/weather/world/city_guides/

Gives the average weather conditions, temperatures, rainfall, and other parameters. A worldwide service providing year-round averages which is easy to understand at a glance.

House matters

www.dbh.govt.nz/tenancy-index

Advice and information for landlords and tenants who rent their homes. The Department of Building and Housing administers the Residential Tenancies Act 1986, receives and holds bonds until the end of a tenancy, and provides dispute-resolution services. Download necessary forms from this site for free.

www.homeforexchange.com

A market place for holiday-home exchange, holiday-home swapping, holiday- and senior-home exchange worldwide.

www.homelinkint.org

A database of homes for exchange: search specific countries and get in touch with exchange partners. Download exchange agreement contracts and get practical advice on house swapping.

Transportation

www.aaroadwatch.ie/eupetrolprices/

Price comparisons between countries for unleaded petrol and diesel. Prices are given in euro and updated monthly. An archive database is also available.

www.theaa.com/allaboutcars/overseas/european_tolls_select.jsp

Information on toll systems that operate in European countries. Specific enough that you can find out how much it will cost you on the A54 or A7 from Montpellier to Aix-en-Provence (it's €8.30 for a car, extra for caravans or trailers). Also covers costs associated with bridges and tunnels.

www.autotrader.co.uk

An online market place for the UK's biggest selection of new and used cars, campervans and caravans, etc. A UK postcode is required for searching purposes, allowing you to find a vehicle in close proximity.

www.theaa.com/arewenearlythereyet/index.html

Beat the travel boredom. Lots of fun games to play in the car (or boat or train, etc.) to pass the time with children. Download PDF files for free and take them with you.

www.momsminivan.com

An American site dedicated to over 101 ideas for fun things for kids to do in the car, kids' travel games, printable car games and activities, and road-trip tips. They are organised by age group.

Families share travel stories

www.familyadventuretravel.co.nz

The Immink family website. Read tales of their travels as they experience all the excitement, highs, lows and dramas that travelling as a family with teenagers brings.

www.france4families.com

A free online travel guide to family holidays in France. Regularly updated, France for Families has been devised by the Harding and King families to express their love of all things French.

www.kidscantravel.com

Suggestions, destinations and holidays for families. Lots of useful advice, plenty of stories from other travelling families, plus an image gallery. Children can watch slide-shows created by other kids, and can create their own travel slide-show to post on this site – really cool!

www.greece4kids.com

A guide for kids going to Greece, written by an eight-year-old girl. A lovely perspective on travelling with your mum and dad. Inspirational. Kids will love this one, especially the pig with the Greek flag in its bottom.

http://homeschooling.gomilpitas.com/weblinks/traveling.htm

With a focus on educating your children while on the road, home school families contribute their stories via forum blogs, articles and videos. Plus there are many useful links to resources pertinent for 'road school'.

Travel blogs and photo-share websites

www.statravelblogs.com/journal/sta/

Create online travel journals, post photos and share your stories. Read blogs from other travellers. A website created by New Zealanders.

www.kodakgallery.com

View and edit your photos, share them with friends, order prints, etc. A way to let family and friends back home see where you are and what you have been doing.

www.flickr.com

Online photographic community where you can create a gallery to share photos with others. Restrictions can be placed on access to protect privacy.

Flights and other deals

www.opodo.co.uk

A search engine for cheap flights and hotels. Includes travel guides.

www.lastminute.com

Search engine for cheap flights, package holidays, entertainment. Good deals to be had at the last minute for stage shows, etc. We saved ourselves a bundle by booking our tickets to Legoland Windsor here.

Documentation

www.passports.govt.nz

Information regarding New Zealand passport rules and regulations, including downloadable forms.

www.mfat.govt.nz

Contact details for all foreign embassies for enquiries regarding visa applications.

www.safetravel.govt.nz

Informative advice on passports, visas and current affairs that can potentially make travel unsafe or unwise. Travel advisories issue risk-level warnings on terrorist activities, political situation, disease outbreaks, flight disruptions and other such circumstances. The things we might have ignored as younger travellers but take more seriously now that we have children.

Internet cafe locations

www.cybercaptive.com

Find the location for net access near you with this online database which contains listings for nearly 6000 verified cybercafes, public internet access points, and internet kiosks in 161 countries.

www.netcafes.com

Similar to Cybercaptive, this site contains a database of more than 4000 internet cafes in 141 countries.

Bibliography

Take Your Kids to Europe: How to Travel Safely (and Sanely) in Europe with Your Children, Cynthia W. Harriman. ISBN: 0-7627-1030-6

One Year Off: Leaving It All Behind for a Round-the-World Journey with Our Children, David Elliot Cohen. ISBN: 1885211651

Allons Enfants – A New Zealand Family in France, Linda Burgess. ISBN-10: 1877135437

Lonely Planet France
Lonely Planet Greece
Lonley Planet Italy
Lonely Planet Portugal
Lonely Planet Spain
Lonely Planet Turkey

Acknowledgments

Thanks a-plenty go to:

Matthew Williamson for holding the fort while we skipped off on our OE and for his fab design skills on this book; Belinda Cooke, Matt Turner and Louise Armstrong at New Holland Publishers for adopting an orphaned author; Bernice Beachman for pointing us in the right direction; Renée Lang for her firm (but fair) hand; all the distant relatives who looked after our wandering family, especially Lynda and Jimmy; all of our friends overseas who put us up, entertained and fed us, and did our laundry – especially the Elliotts, Pritchards and Franklins; the wonderful Immink family for input to the book and being new buddies; our friends back home who make the return worthwhile; Jeremy Shanahan for being a cool travel agent; Iain and Cathy Fraser for reading the draft; Jan and Norm for looking after our 'treasures' and letting their 'little girl' go away yet again; Mary and Miles; Steve, Ro and their girls for letting us camp at their house; Jeannie for being Luke for a year; Karey, Lucy and Hayley for looking after pets; and ASB bank who made it all so financially easy and credit card fraud a lot less painful.

*Sunset in the Midlands
and the twilight weeks
of our trip. Out exploring
with new English friends.*

Fishing off a bridge in Istanbul, Turkey.
Karen and her camera receiving wary
looks from the men.

Index